Thinking of ...

Buying a Cloud Solution?

Ask the Smart Questions

By Ian Gotts & Stephen Parker

Smart Questions™ Philosophy

Smart Questions is built on 4 key pillars, which set it apart from other publishers:

1. *Smart people want Smart Questions not Dumb Answers*
2. *Domain experts are often excluded from authorship, so we are making writing a book simple and painless*
3. *The community has a great deal to contribute to enhance the content*
4. *We donate a percentage of revenue to a charity voted for by the authors and the community. It is great marketing, but it is also the right thing to do*

www.Smart-Questions.com

Reviews

Cloud Computing is a new business model that requires new thinking for our customers. How they architect the solution, how they secure the applications and how they federate their on-premise computing with the cloud are all extremely critical success factors for Cloud Computing adoption. Ian and Stephen have done a great job of exposing the questions that our customers need to be asking their cloud services vendors to ensure a successful project.

Shannon Day, Marketing Manager Software plus Services (Microsoft, www.microsoft.com)

This is one of the most valuable and informative technology books for professionals that I have read. Finally the mystery of "Cloud Computing" has been solved. This is a must read for anyone in IT or in a management position within a business that is considering or wants to know the straight facts about Cloud Computing. A good common sense review of what Cloud Computing is and is not, coupled with a detailed list of questions to help you decide on the right approach for your particular needs.

Toby Tarczy, Managing Director (Calvella, www.calvella.com)

This book parts the clouds on an exciting and inevitable evolution of information services and the way we work and play. It reminds all of us that the devil is in the detail and that the benefits to be realized, which are many, are won through effective planning and preparation and the effective execution of the implementation plan. Above all the book is practical, insightful and pragmatic. It will look strangely familiar to anyone experienced in managing change in systems and organizations. It is a valuable resource as its cuts through the mystery and explains it in plain language.

David E Alexander, Managing Director (Solutions Make The Difference, www.solutionsmtd.com)

There are many sources of information, but not one source for all the information that buyers need to conduct their evaluation of Cloud Computing. Until now that is – "Thinking of... Buying Cloud Computing? Ask the Smart Questions" puts buyers in the driving seat. Caveat Emptor becomes Caveat Venditor!

Frank Bennett, Founder (SaaSDeal, www.saasdeal.co.uk)

Authors

Ian Gotts

Founder and CEO of Nimbus, which has been offering their process management solution as a Cloud Computing offering to major corporations for the last 4 years. This was a transition made from the traditional model. Now over 70% of new customers have used the Nimbus service including Toyota, SAP, Cognos, Nestle, HM Revenue & Customs and HSBC Bank.

He is author of 2 books, Common Approach, Uncommon Results and Why Killer Products Don't Sell which makes him a sought after conference speaker. He is an active investor in technology companies which make business sense.

Stephen Parker

A business executive, with over 20 years experience of taking critical technology investment decisions and delivering solutions on the leading edge of IT in large enterprises, ".com" start-ups, and business turnarounds. His recent journey of turning around a struggling ERP vendor into a leading Cloud Computing business in the eProcurement space and taking this to a trade sale has added scars and knowledge in equal measures.

His down to earth approach, backed up by real-life experience provides him with a rare insight into the world of Cloud Computing. He is kept busy providing consulting services to companies considering Cloud Computing and to analyst firms focused in this space as well as speaking and writing on the subject.

Table of Contents

Acknowledgements

No business book which has any realism or personality is possible without the generous contributions of companies who are prepared to open up old wounds to allow others to learn from their mistakes. So our thanks go to them.

And to those who invented the internet which made the Smart Questions approach possible

Foreword

Cloud Computing is evolving at a great pace. Some would say maturing. But the shape and scope is still not clear and the potential is still largely untapped. We see Cloud Computing driving business transformation in corporations, in a way that mirrors the changes in behavior that we've already seen in consumers. The era of "any place, any time, anywhere" is being ushered in by stunning, innovative Web2.0 applications running on highly scalable infrastructure powered by the IT heavyweights. The final piece in the puzzle is reliable connectivity.

The potential of launching new companies or new ideas, delivering exceptional business value is staggering. And the speed that they can be brought to market is like nothing we have seen before. In a world where unlimited finance is no longer available, the ability to scale a company is not necessarily directly tied to working capital. These new solutions will help established corporations transform and free their employees from the daily commute to offices with desks, computers and internal systems. Maybe it is too much to hope that this will reduce global warming and enable people to get the work-life back in balance. But it is a good start.

But with any change there is risk. Financial risk, business risk, reputational risk. Risk is not bad. It comes with the territory. What is bad is unrecognized and unmanaged risk. That is why this book is so valuable. It is the list of places to look for risk. Reading it may make you feel depressed about the potential of Cloud Computing and scared of even approaching it. That is the wrong reaction. The beauty of this book is that it lists all the concerns that you could possibly have – although not all of them will be relevant to your situation.

Ian and Stephen have pulled together a great book on the subject of purchasing Cloud Computing and brought it to life with some fabulous anecdotes. My plea to you is to read the book, think carefully about the Smart Questions and use them to make equally smart decisions in your organization. And make sure that you are not one of the horror stories in the next edition of the book.

Darren Bibby (Program Director, IDC Software Channels Research)

Who should read this book?

People like you and me

This book is not technical, nor was it ever intended to be. It is aimed squarely at those who see IT as a utility that should be consumed to serve the business. Not the reverse. People like you and me.

This book is intended to be a catalyst for action aimed at a range of people inside and outside your organization. Here are just a few, and why it is relevant to them:

Chief Executive Officer

As CEO you are responsible for the overall performance of the business. That means setting strategy and that includes considering Cloud Computing. You are probably aware of Cloud Computing as a term. You can probably bet that your business managers or IT team are looking at it as an option to increase availability, increase flexibility or reduce cost.

Understanding the Smart Questions will allow you to be better prepared when they present their business case.

Chief Executive Officer of a start-up

You are probably looking at Cloud Computing as a way of delivering all your IT systems. But is it the right long term strategy? What are the risks inherent in this strategy? Will it support or hamper your speed to market and your long term growth?

This book will help you ask the Smart Questions, because if you don't it may cost you the company.

Chief Operations Officer

Cloud Computing could change the way you run the operation. It could give you more freedom. It could enable remote working which will reduce travel costs, improve your carbon footprint, reduce staff churn, improve employee morale – or possibly it will just make the place even more difficult to run.

Asking the Smart Questions, so that you get the right answers, will help you assess the impact of Cloud Computing.

Chief Finance Officer

They say Cloud Computing is cheaper. So it sounds like a no brainer. Or is it? As CFO you are also expected to safeguard the company from a risk and governance perspective. How do you balance the potential cost savings vs. the other factors? What metrics do you need to put in place to ensure success?

This book will give you a sound understanding of the areas to question.

Chief Information Officer / Chief Technical Officer

Cloud Computing is squarely in your court. But just because you are responsible for IT strategy for the company doesn't necessarily mean that you understand the all nuances of Cloud Computing. But you do need to understand enough to be able to control and manage major projects to budget and time. That could include the move to Cloud Computing. So, think of this book as the 3 Rs:

1. Some of the questions will be in areas where you know all the answers so they will be **Reinforced** in your mind.

2. You may have forgotten certain areas so the book will **Remind** you.

3. And other questions may be things you've never considered and will be **Revealed** to you[1].

Sales Director

Your people are constantly on the road and don't or won't update customer and sales records. They are using the excuse that they can't access your customer system unless they are in the office, and they should be out visiting customers not doing admin. Cloud Computing seems the perfect answer. Perhaps too perfect?

This book will help you understand the implications of Cloud Computing, and the right questions to ask.

---

[1] Hint: Don't look surprised and no-one will ever know.

Services Director

You have similar problems to the Sales Director. Your delivery consultants are either at customers or at home. Rarely in the office, they need access to customer information whilst on the move. So is Cloud Computing the only option? And what are the trade-offs?

This book will help you understand the implications of Cloud Computing, and the right questions to ask.

HR Director

Cloud Computing will enable you to work in very different ways. As an organization you can be more flexible and responsive. But are these benefits achievable with current HR policies and practices. How much do they need to or are able to change?

The book will help you understand what questions to ask and how.

Line of business manager

You've seen the system or service which fits your business needs perfectly. It is available right now, which is far, far faster than your internal IT can normally deliver. The pricing is compelling, within your sign-off limits and can come out of budgets that do not require IT sign-off or protracted procurement. In short – you want it NOW.

This book will help you avoid career limiting pitfalls which could catch you out once the system or service has been implemented and the IT department has found out.

How to use this book

This book is intended to be the catalyst for action. We hope that the ideas and examples inspire you to act. So, do whatever you need to do to make this book useful. Use Post-it notes, photocopy pages, scan pages, and write on it. Go to our website and email colleagues the e-book summary. Rip it apart, or read it quickly in one sitting. Whatever works for you. We hope this becomes your most dog-eared book.

Clever clogs – skip to the questions

Some of you understand the background to Cloud Computing and have a pretty good grasp of the implications, benefits and risks. Therefore you have permission to skip to Chapter 6 where the structure of the questions is explained.

But before you go, please read "Getting Involved" on the next page. You can always come back to Chapters 1-5 later.

Getting Involved

The Smart Questions community

There may be questions that we should have asked but didn't. Or specific questions which may be relevant to your situation, but not everyone in general. Go to the website for the book (*www.Smart-Questions.com*) and post the questions. You never know, they may make it into the next edition of the book. That is a key part of the Smart Questions Philosophy.

Send us your feedback

We love feedback. We prefer great reviews, but we'll accept anything that helps take the ideas further. We welcome your comments on this book.

We'd prefer email, as it's easy to answer and saves trees. If the ideas worked for you, we'd love to hear your success stories. Maybe we could turn them into 'Talking Heads'-style video or audio interviews on our website, so others can learn from you. That's one of the reasons why we wrote this book. So talk to us.

feedback@Smart-Questions.com

Got a book you need to write?

Maybe you are a domain expert with knowledge locked up inside you. You'd love to share it and there are people out there desperate for your insights. But you don't think you are an author and don't know where to start. Making it easy for you to write a book is part of the Smart Questions Philosophy.

Let us know about your book idea, and let's see if we can help you get your name in print.

potentialauthor@Smart-Questions.com

Chapter

Big reward equals high risk?

Twenty years from now you will be more disappointed by the things that you didn't do than by the ones you did do. So throw off the bowlines. Sail away from the safe harbor. Catch the trade winds in your sails. Explore. Dream. Discover

Mark Twain (American author, 1835 - 1910)

Head in the Clouds

IT seemed to be a no-brainer. We could swap out our clunky home-grown system and be up and running in days with a new CRM solution. Better still, we didn't need to deal with our internal IT department who just 'love to say No'.

The business case stacked up. We did all the background checks on the vendor's website and made some reference calls to customers in similar businesses to our own. Getting access to the service was really straightforward and the vendor's support team was first class.

So where did it all go wrong?

One of our major Government customers performed a routine audit and discovered that the data held on them in our new CRM system, which we proudly showed them, is held on servers outside the country. And this breaches some law or policy or something. They didn't give us specifics. But they were very clear about the consequences. We've been struck off their Preferred Vendor List, destroying 5 years of hard work and investment by our Public Sector team. The team is now suicidal.

Cloud Computing: a definition

Cloud Computing is the in-vogue name for the model of providing software from a remote location, over a network, where the organization using the software does not have to be involved with the day to day running of it.

It clearly has great benefits, but also comes with risks[2]. But not all the risks are that obvious hence the need for this book. But first we need to agree some definitions.

Originally the generally accepted term was Software as a Service. The use of the word service was based on the association with other "services" that we just use without being concerned about the complexities behind the scenes e.g. the telephone, the supply of electricity, the use of our Visa card.

As more people have started writing about and promoting the approach there has been an SAE[3] making it difficult to differentiate between SaaS, PaaS, S+S, DaaS, ASP, On-Demand or Utility. So in this book we are going to use "Cloud Computing" which seems to be the umbrella term that is gaining traction and is being used almost universally. The new term is based on the services being provided by servers which are in the Cloud.

Terminology

There are many terms being bandied around to describe this approach. Below are just some of them:

- SaaS : Software as a Service

- PaaS : Platform as a Service

- ASP : Application Service Provider

- Hosted

- Software + Services : On-premise software + hosted services

- On-Demand

- Web 2.0

- Utility Computing

We will be using "Cloud Computing" as a generic umbrella term for all of these.

---

[2] No such thing as a free lunch etc etc

[3] SAE - Significant Acronym Explosion!

The opposite of this approach is referred to as on-premise, where, as the name suggests the hardware and software are installed and run within an organization. Today this is still by some way the dominant approach.

There is a long history of the IT industry providing models where software can be delivered as a service from a central location, and one could even argue that this goes right back to the mainframe days (plus ca change, plus c'est la meme chose). Terms such as eBusiness, on demand, utility computing, ASP and so forth have been marketed since the mid 90's, all with the same basic message that you should not have to worry about looking after the infrastructure for delivering your software, you should just get on and use it.

Naturally as time has passed, refinements are being offered to this simple, everything "On-Premise" or everything "in the Cloud" story. Microsoft in particular has advocated the concept of a hybrid model that they refer to as Software plus Services. The idea is that the best solutions will combine the benefits of on-premise software with the advantages of services delivered via the web.

And whilst this may have started as marketing or positioning, in reality it is really the logical architectural approach, given that the mobile workforce cannot guarantee being connected 100% of the time.

Cloud Computing is evolving and there is a growing list of synonyms to cover various elements of the paradigm. One is the notion of "Multi Tenant" architecture for the software. This is the concept of one installation of the software having many customers using it, each with their data and configuration segregated by the software. Like a building with multiple self-contained apartments with multiple tenants. However this is not the only approach. Virtualization allows many installations of a standard "application environment" on the same physical server, allowed a "virtual dedicated" environment per customer.

The future is here

Some say that the future is already here, but it is unevenly distributed.

Big reward equals high risk?

By that we mean that if you look around you can find examples of any new innovation being used in anger, delivering business benefits, it's just that not everyone is using it. A recent survey by Information Age highlighted the top 10 Cloud Computing systems. What is interesting is that they are currently all 100% hosted. None of them has any locally installed software.

Whilst this may be the best route for some systems, and is certainly the ideal answer for a consumer system, it is not necessarily best for an enterprise customer. They may require the local processing power of a PC for some analytical or reporting, but also the system needs to recognize when users are not connected and allow them to continue working, albeit with slightly reduced functionality.

Information Age Top 10 Web 2.0 apps

Information Age in October 2008 listed its view of the best 10 Web 2.0 apps, and here they are:

Coca Cola: The drink maker's exhaustive use of Web 2.0 keeps its brand in front of young eyes

Best Buy: Electronics retailer has built an exemplary internal social network

Ernst & Young: Facebook-based recruitment program lets the accounting giant keep in touch with the finest graduates

Procter & Gamble: Retail manufacturer's BeingGirl website built a community around a brand that was otherwise tricky to market to

Wachovia Bank: A web 2.0-powered intranet is tackling some of the US bank's biggest issues

Dell: IdeaStorm lets the computer maker's customers contribute to innovation

GE: The US giant has evolved a collaboration framework that has revolutionized knowledge management

Elsevier: Scientific publisher incorporates community into its information services

IBM: Web 2.0 software allows Big Blue to get its 300,000 employees together in global 'Jam' events

PlusNet: Innovative Internet service vendor lets its customer do the support work.

Email

We all have access to email, but rarely stop to consider the complex technical architecture behind it which enables you to have hundreds of emails offering Viagra or "body enhancement" pumped to you daily - wherever you are. I can access my email on-line through a secure web page using any browser. I can access it using Outlook on my PC in either on-line or off-line mode. I can access email using the light or mobile version of Outlook, again in on-line or off-line mode. And all these ways of accessing a single email stay in sync. Now I've looked at an email which has been downloaded onto my mobile, it should also be available through a web page using a browser at an airport kiosk.

Salesforce.com & Force.com

Often held up as the poster child for Cloud Computing, it was not the first, nor is it the largest. It is a significant company with great reach, a compelling vision which has only starting to play out with its development platform. What made it the poster child for Cloud Computing was its powerful PR and the original tagline of "No software". That line is not really true now. To get the most out of the core CRM system you need to be connected, but there is the ability to work offline with locally installed software either on the PC or the mobile device.

What is making salesforce.com's long term potential as one of the major software players so exciting is Force.com. Force.com has "drag and drop" tools that allow a business-user to build a new business system (such as HR or Operations). It has a development environment where systems engineers can code complex logic, validation, workflow and screen designs to make that simple business system come to life. And it provides all this through a hosted platform.

Microsoft Azure

Microsoft is often accused of coming late to any party. What they cannot be faulted for is the immense investment that they are prepared to make once they decide to join the party, and how patient they are to get a result. Microsoft Azure is their "Cloud Computing platform in the sky" enabling anyone with a correctly designed Microsoft application to run it from the "Cloud" for their customers. This is taking away the risk and investment for a start-up wanting to deploy a system at scale. It has the potential to be game changing for the software development marketplace.

Google

They are shaking up the enterprise world of IT by offering their hosted systems such as email and office systems (word processing, spreadsheets, presentation) to corporations. And lots are taking a serious look. The price, or lack of price, is making it compelling. And just as people were questioning whether the inability to work on documents when you were not connected would be a barrier, Google offered an offline option through their Google Gears technology. If nothing else it is driving some interesting discussions on pricing.

Twitter & twittersphere

Love it, hate it, or simply don't understand it[4]. Twitter.com relies on you being connected 100% of the time as it is a 100% web based solution. But an ecosystem of partners has sprung up around Twitter to provide partial-connectivity solutions. You can send a tweet (post a 140 character Twitter entry) as an SMS from your mobile phone. You can download systems to your mobile phone which enable you to tweet. There are PC apps which will allow you to compose a tweet and are happy working offline and then syncing when you are back online.

Running as a Cloud Computing service from day one it has been able to scale as the demand has grown (not without some pains as any user of Twitter will tell you). And springing up all around it are other startups which add additional analysis capabilities. Most of which are 100% hosted, but not all. There are desktop or mobile apps which are installed on a device with web service calls to the central database held in the Cloud by Twitter.

---

[4] If you don't understand it there are some great videos – or just join and start tweeting

Chapter

Why me and why now?

Don't wait the time will never be right.

Napoleon Hill (Author, 1883 – 1970)

S O why should I be interested? The Cloud Computing evangelists would have us all believe that this is the only future and someday soon all software will be delivered as a service. And looking at the huge investments that some of the largest "gorillas" in the IT industry are making, maybe there is something to this. However putting on one side the hyperbole that always goes hand in hand with new ideas in IT, there are in fact many sound reasons to consider this approach.

Enterprise capability at commodity costs

By providing the service to multiple customers, utilizing a common centralized infrastructure and multi-tenancy, the vendor can achieve economies of scale and therefore provide the service at a reduced cost compared to an on-premise solution. Also by "outsourcing" the service provision there will be the potential for internal cost savings.

However, this requires a huge investment in capabilities that typically go beyond what a business (especially SME's) could afford to or would want to deploy. For example, redundant servers, on-site spares, multiple data centers supporting disaster recovery, 24 hr security guards, enterprise versions of software (rather than standard), a team of technical specialists, sophisticated backup etc

etc. And yet due to the economies of scale available by sharing this infrastructure across multiple customers, this is still offered at commodity costs.

Amazon: retailer or infrastructure vendor?

Amazon was one of the few companies launched in the dotcom era that has made it. They are an example of selling the 'Long Tail' which the internet has made possible and financially viable. But they are 100% on-line. No internet connection means no access.

As an e-commerce site they need to have the computing capacity to cope with peaks in demand, such as the last minute Christmas purchases. As this capacity is largely unused during other times, they have launched a service called EC2, "Elastic Cloud Computing". Put simply, they are making their servers available, at a cost, for anyone who has an application that they want run from the Cloud. So processing, memory, storage and bandwidth wrapped up in an availability, serviceability and maintainability set of processes all for a scalable fee off a rate card.

Freed from the financial constraints of purchasing servers, connectivity, back-up and all the supporting costs we should expect to see very innovative companies launching using Amazon as the platform. But don't expect them to be large and well-funded. This new model means that a very capable looking system could be two guys in the dorm room at college. So don't be surprised if support is only available when they are not in lectures or out partying.

This basic concept is nothing new, with a long tradition of businesses outsourcing non-core activities to third parties who can offer reduced costs due to their economies of scale. After all how many companies run their own postal, telecommunications, transportation or electricity services?

It took electricity 60 years to move to the Cloud model; why should software be any different?

A hundred years ago, companies stopped generating their own power with steam engines and dynamos and plugged into the newly built electric grid. The cheap power pumped out by electric utilities didn't just change how businesses operate. It set off a chain reaction of economic and social transformations that brought the modern world into existence. Today, a similar revolution is under way. Hooked up to the Internet's global computing grid, massive information-processing plants have begun pumping data and software code into our homes and businesses. This time, it's computing that's turning into a utility.

Summary of "The Big Switch" by Nicholas Carr

Speed of availability

Because the service is already installed and waiting for use, much of the traditional time taken to plan, install, configure and deploy is removed. This can allow businesses to have rapid access to sophisticated services and start achieving the business benefits as soon as possible. But don't confuse availability with your own ability to use the service. There will be changes in the way you work. There will be manual activities. There may be specific ways that you want the service used. Simply making the service available, unless it is very simple and of a very narrow scope, will result in chaos. Do you want every person entering data or using features in a different way?

Anywhere Access

Due to the centralized nature of the service, it no longer matters where you are as long as you can access the internet (at least occasionally). Sophisticated mobile devices (Blackberry, Windows Mobile etc.) have further pushed this idea by providing access to email and company data wherever you are in the world.

The hybrid models such as Software plus Services are also providing answers to the "what happens if I am not connected to the internet" question by providing synchronized copies of your data, which is managed centrally by the "service", to your local device's "software".

Always up to date

The centralized management of the services makes it easier for the vendor to deploy updates and once deployed all users will have access to the new capabilities. This also provides the opportunity to have more frequent release cycles, which leads to a more rapid introduction of improvements, bug fixes and customer enhancement requests.

> ## Salesforce.com: A new day and what new functionality has appeared?
>
> When salesforce.com first launched in the UK, for early customers the service was a fairly basic CRM solution; accounts, contacts, opportunities and reporting. But that was perfect. Most customers were migrating from using Outlook and they were small.
>
> But salesforce.com had grander ambitions and had a development team back in San Francisco working hard to extend the functionality. Therefore each new release meant that users would come in to discover new tabs had appeared, such as campaigns, or a few new fields in the contacts tabs or new screen designs. No warning, no ability to preview and test. Bang, it was there. A true big-bang implementation.
>
> Now salesforce.com is far more sophisticated and mature. You have the ability to control which tabs and fields an end user sees and the screen layouts. There is a sandbox for testing prior to making new functionality available. That means that customers now control the implementation of new functionality, not salesforce.com. But salesforce.com still gets the benefit of providing one code base to all users around the world.
>
> This requires a far more sophisticated system than the one first launched 5 years ago. Fortunately, salesforce.com is now a mature and capable service.

This is in sharp contrast to the traditional on-premise model with one or maybe two updates a year and many customers not deploying these updates due to the business disruption and overhead involved and hence not receiving the benefits of the new release.

Maturity

Although there is always room for improvement, the reliability, security and capability of the "Cloud services" is in general "good enough". As the music industry has found to its surprise, people have been happy to accept the quality compromises of the portable MP3 format, because of the huge gains in convenience and reduced cost[5]. The presence of industry heavy weights such as Google, IBM, Microsoft et al, further reinforces the validity of the market. Maturity will come.

---

[5] I'm not suggesting free (ripped), but buying by the track, rather than an entire CD

Music trends show the impact of the web on record company's business models

The music industry has grown accustomed to dismal sales numbers, and in 2008 even the good news comes with disappointment. "Tha Carter III" is the first release in SoundScan's 17-year history to top the year-end list with sales of fewer than 3 million.

Sales of digital music continued to rise steeply. Just over a billion songs were downloaded, a 27 percent increase from 2007, and some record companies say they are finally beginning to wring significant profits from music on Web sites like YouTube and MySpace. But analysts say that despite the growth and promise of digital music — in 2003 just 19 million songs were purchased as downloads — the money made online is still far from enough to make up for losses in physical sales.

"As the digital side grows, you get a different business model, with more revenue streams," said Michael McGuire, an analyst with Gartner, a market research firm. "But do we get back to where the revenue that the labels see is going to be fully replacing the CD in the next four to five years? No." Gartner recently issued a report urging record companies to put their primary focus on downloads.

Why me and why now?

Chapter

3

Timing is everything

Timing has a lot to do with the outcome of the rain dance.

Cowboy proverb

G IVEN the earlier comments, an obvious question is, "Why is now the right time for the 'service' based software delivery model to succeed?" There are many reasons, some of which are technical, but most are emotional which is often the key barrier to change.

Markets

Costs

The UK and other western countries have for some time been migrating to a knowledge economy, with the need to compete globally and increasingly with low cost economies. This has provided the impetus for solutions that offer low cost, global reach for both the customers and the software vendor.

The lowered cost base has also opened up the opportunity to market and sell to the "long tail" and this is driving new business models within companies both large and small (Google, eBay, Amazon, Microsoft, Salesforce et al). The success of these businesses is in turn encouraging further adoption.

Availability

Before, there were a limited number of systems that were available from anywhere in the world. That is no longer true. Pretty much everything you want to do – from email to storing and sharing

M&A legal documentation, booking someone to decorate your home whilst you are on holiday, to printing books, are now available online. They may be provided by a one-man band sitting in a bedroom above a pizza delivery kitchen which is probably not ideal if they are going to be strategic to your operation, or they may be a global software vendor. But by simply looking at their website you cannot tell.

Audience

Expectations

People are now used to having access to sophisticated and reliable service offerings at home to manage their email (Hotmail, Gmail etc), social networks (Facebook), online purchases (Amazon), gaming (Xbox Live) and even commerce (eBay), without the requirement for "complex IT". This social acceptance of the technology at home is in turn informing the debate at the office about why business cannot have access to reliable, easy to use, low cost (or even free) services.

Setting standards

Even up to the year 2000 the only technology that many people touched was at work. The equipment and the system – the UX (User eXperience) was provided by your employer. Now Bill Gates vision of "a computer in every home" is nearly realized (within countries such as the UK), and so individual's expectations are being set by the websites and systems they access at home for social networking, for e-commerce and for watching video and listening to music. Those innovative websites do not necessarily have to have the levels of resilience which a corporate system needs. Also they are likely to be more fun than entering Sales Order information or processing an Accounting transaction into an ERP solution. But they are setting a standard against which corporate systems are being judged.

iPod generation

New generations of end users are emerging from schools and colleges. They have grown up around technology that is now ubiquitous. It has driven a very different lifestyle and expectation, and many of the technologies have emerged since the year 2000:

- Everyone has a mobile phone from the age of 10. Advances in processing power, battery life, screen resolution, available systems and low cost talk plans have made it possible to use it as the universal communicator (voice, email, Instant Messaging), a media center (music, video stored or streamed), a games machine, and a micro-computer running systems.

- Internet access is available in most homes so consumers have become accustomed to a very rich internet experience (Web 2.0). This has set an expectation for business systems.

- Social networking sites and MMP (massively multi-player) computer games have changed the way they interact, communicate and play with their peers. Their confidence and trust of the internet and the way they evaluate others they meet on the internet is very different from the traditional face to face meeting. They bare their souls, quirks, passions and fetishes on social networking sites, but they would never reveal them in a job interview.

- Internet search (Google, Yahoo, Microsoft), Wikipedia and a plethora of website, blogs, podcasts and video sharing sites means that information is a couple of clicks away: "how to do something", "where to go", "cheapest place to buy". It has also changed the way that they learn.

- Every one of them seems to have little white earphones permanently inserted in their ears; even when they are working, when they need to concentrate, if they are on the phone or out in a group of friends.

Technology is only technology if it was invented after you were born

An interesting insight comes from the research from Don Tapscott's book, "grown up digital". If you grew up with a service then it is not new technology to "learn". For Generation X the TV, phone or electricity are not technology. They just use them. So, for the iPod Generation, Generation Y, the internet and mobile social networking are not technology. The iPod generation is growing up expecting to use these services, not 'learn or understand how they work'.

Capability

Always-on

Finally we have the technical environment that has underpinned this change. Without doubt the most significant driver has been the mass availability of low cost, reliable broadband. This has made reliable, high speed access to the internet achievable for all businesses and most homes. But it is not always-on. A quick train ride across the UK shows that even the mobile phone service is patchy at best. So maybe we should term it 'nearly always-on at-rest' i.e. when stationary. In most major cities and towns you should be able to find a Wi-Fi connection – even if only in a Starbucks. Expect this to change dramatically over the next 2-5 years until the entire city has Wi-Fi connectivity either through hot-spots or through far better mobile phone coverage.

Infrastructure

To launch a Cloud Computing service it used to mean that the vendor needed to provide the servers, bandwidth, disk storage etc. yourself. This was a huge barrier to entry for start-ups and why VC's had a key (and very profitable) role to play in the Dot Com revolution. However this is no longer true, with an embarrassment of choice for hosting partners, such as Amazon, Microsoft, Google and others. Web 2.0 start ups are being launched at a ferocious rate with 3F[6] seed funding.

Software availability

Supporting all of this has been the rapid development of technical standards for data transfer, connectivity and development frameworks, and whilst as always there are competing "camps", the core standards are common (XML, web services, AJAX et al). There has also been a commoditization of core services (data centers, telecoms, server hardware), and the availability of "off the shelf" software components that support multi-tenanted deployment.

---

[6] Family, friends and fanatics

Mass customization

Services are also now being designed to allow for mass customization through configuration i.e. each customer can configure the service to their specific needs, but the service vendor only has to manage a single common code base. This has helped to bridge the gap between a "vanilla" service that may be cheap, but is just too standard to be useful and solutions that are highly customized and unique to each customer, with the associated costs.

Timing is everything

Chapter
4

Too good to be true?

Your mind is like water. When it becomes agitated it becomes difficult to see. But if you let it settle the answer becomes clear.

Master Ugwe (Turtle, Kung Fu Panda, 2008)

ALTHOUGH there are many potential advantages of having your software delivered as a service (whether Software as a Service or a hybrid such as Software plus Services), it is still a maturing delivery model and as such there are potential gotchas[7]. Understanding these risks and controlling, or at least mitigating the risks, is critical to benefiting from the potential of Cloud Computing.

Understanding the risks

The Existing Software Ecosystem & Skills

Despite all the hype the dominant delivery model for software is still the on-premise one. This means that the majority of IT workers and those that can support your business will be familiar with and experienced in managing software on your premises.

Reliability and Security

When your software is delivered from a remote location you may never physically see the facilities used to deliver the service. Although things are improving and industry standards evolving,

---

[7] As we said earlier, there is no such thing as a free lunch

there is little to stop a vendor from taking shortcuts to save costs and hoping that problems do not occur.

Security especially, is a complex area to get right and can easily be overlooked or ignored.

Offline Access

In a pure "only in the Cloud" computing model the service is only available when you are connected to the internet, so how do I work when I am offline? And you are offline a lot, especially if you travel by train in the UK.

Data Ownership

With the global availability of the internet, the location of the data center where your data is stored may not be within your country or even geographic area. This may affect the rights of the local authorities to have access to your data, or to whether you actually retain title to your data at all.

Commercial Arrangements

The traditional on-premise world was simple, you paid for a perpetual license for your software and some form of optional annual "support and maintenance" agreement. You provided the hardware and networks and probably you used some external consultants to install and implement the software. And after that is was your problem to manage. But the vast majority of the costs were up-front as part of the implementation project.

With Cloud Computing things are changing fast. The offerings are maturing and although there are some common threads, there are also many loose ends. There are different charging models varying from free or ad-funded with little or no support through to managed services with on-going annual, quarterly or monthly costs.

Maturing and changing marketplace

It is important to recognize that this is a rapidly maturing marketplace. Things that were complex, high value services yesterday could well be low cost commodities tomorrow. As the market has matured so the early adopting, small business entrepreneurs have been joined by the industry gorillas and this in turn has driven the cost models downwards for the core services.

CRM is a classic example, where until recently businesses could spend tens or hundreds of thousands or even millions of pounds deploying systems from companies such as Seibel. Now companies such as salesforce.com and more recently Microsoft are offering alternative service offerings, based on a "per user", "per month", commodity pricing model.

Enterprise level scalability and integration

A quickly hacked together mashup may look good at first blush, but will it scale? During recent snowstorms in the UK an enterprising developer overnight created "UK Snow" which was a mashup of Twitter and Google maps. It delivered a real time service for the UK and was more up to date than Met office.

But for enterprise scale applications a well thought through architecture is required to ease the management of change, servicing, maintenance, upgrading components without service disruption and enabling management control to be aligned to business needs.

So should I leave well alone?

It is no good asking the vendor generic questions and accepting a tick box YES from a tender, on the assumption that if they are being "economical with the truth" you can sue them later. By then you will have invested time and crucially business disruption and will effectively be tied in. Unfortunately the IT industry (along with many others) is quite happy to say yes and then after the sale protest their innocence by claiming "if only you had told me you meant….". The harsh reality is CAVEAT EMPTOR (let the buyer beware).

So, with this in mind, should you give Cloud Computing a wide berth? It depends. Everything we do in business (and life) carries a risk. The key is to understand the risks that we are taking, so we can make informed decisions and put the appropriate risk management strategies in place. Understanding the risks and your ability to manage them, may make a service based approach wrong for you, or it may be the answer to a maiden's prayer and reduce existing risks within your business. Critically however, there is a fundamental difference between risk management and risk aversion, with the later typically leading to stagnation, decay and failure.

To understand the risks, you need to make sure you ask the Smart Questions, both internally and of your vendors.

Chapter

Ask the Smart Questions

If I have seen further it is by standing on the shoulders of giants.

Isaac Newton (Scientist, 1643 – 1727)

SMART Questions are about giving you valuable insights or "the Smarts". Normally these are only gained through years of painful and costly experience. Whether you already have a general understanding of the subject and need to take it to the next level or are starting from scratch, you need to make sure you ask the Smart Questions. And the ideal time to "Ask the Smart Questions" is while you are still "Thinking of...." and not as a response to problems after you have jumped. We aim to short circuit that learning process, by providing the expertise of the 'giants' that Isaac Newton referred to.

Not all the questions will necessarily be new or staggeringly insightful. The value you get from the information will clearly vary. It depends on your job role and previous experience. We call this the 3Rs.

The 3 Rs

1. Some of the questions will be in areas where you know all the answers so they will be **Reinforced** in your mind.

2. You may have forgotten certain areas so the book will **Remind** you.

3. And other questions may be things you've never considered and will be **Revealed** to you.

How do you use Smart Questions?

The structure of the questions is set out in Chapter 6, and the questions are laid out in tables in Chapters 7 and 8. In the table you have the basic question and then the reason why you should care. We've also provided a helpful checkbox so that you can mark which questions are relevant to your particular situation.

A quick scan down the list of questions should give you a general feel of where you are for each question vs. the 3Rs[8].

At the highest level they are a sanity check or checklist of areas to consider. You can take them with you to meetings or use as the basis of your ITT[9]. Just one question may save you a whole heap of cash or heartache.

In Chapter 9 we've tried to bring some of the questions to life with some real-life examples.

There may be some 'aha' moments. Hopefully not too many sickening, 'head in the hands – what have we done' moments, where you've realized that you company is hopelessly exposed. If you're in that situation, then the questions will help you negotiate yourself back into control.

In this context, probably the most critical role of the questions is that they reveal risks that you hadn't considered. Risks that could seriously damage your business as we described in the opening chapter. On the flip side they should open up your thinking to opportunities that you hadn't necessarily considered. Balancing the opportunities and the risks, and then agreeing what is realistically achievable is the key to formulating strategy.

The questions could be used in your internal operational meetings to inform or at least prompt the debate. Alternatively they could shape the discussion you have with the potential vendors of Cloud Computing services.

Once that strategy is set, the questions should enable you to develop costed operational plans, develop budgets or determine IT strategy.

---

[8] Or whether you need the For Dummies book (which we haven't written)

[9] Invitation To Tender, like RFP (Request for Proposal)

How to dig deeper

Need more information? Not convinced by the examples, or want ones that are more relevant to you specific situation? The Smart Questions micro-site for the book has a list of other supporting material. As this subject is moving quickly many of the links are to websites or blogs.

And of course there is a community of people who've read the book and are all at different levels of maturity who have been brought together on the Smart Questions micro-site for the book.

And finally

Please remember that these questions are NOT intended to be a prescriptive list that must be followed slavishly from beginning to end. It is inevitable that the list of questions is not exhaustive and we are confident that with the help of the community the list of Smart Questions will grow.

If you want to rephrase a question to improve its context or have identified a question we've missed, then let us know and add to the collective knowledge.

We also understand that not all of the questions will apply to all businesses. However we encourage you to read them all as there may be a nugget of truth that can be adapted to your circumstances.

Above all we hope that this book provides a guide or a pointer to the areas that may be valuable to you and helps with the "3 Rs".

Chapter 6

Cloud Computing Questions

Any time, any place, anywhere.

Martini drinks advert (1970 – 1980s)

CLOUD Computing is all about providing information to the individual wherever they happen to be, whatever they are doing, and in a format that they want to consume it. Oh – and at an acceptable level of risk and cost to the company.

So that is the backdrop for these questions. What do I need to know to quantify the costs, opportunities and risks, and then manage the risks?

The questions have been grouped into the following structure:

Chapter 7: Questions for my own organization?

1. **Why are we considering Cloud Computing?** These are questions around the benefits and opportunities that are achievable. What is motivating you?

2. **What do we need from the service?** These are about your organization's business and technical needs.

3. **What are the costs?** Where are the internal costs of implementing Cloud Computing?

4. **What are the external barriers?** There will be external limitations; legal, contractual, or physical that will need to be addressed. Some may be deal-breakers.

5. **Are we ready internally?** What are all the activities that need to happen to fully exploit Cloud Computing? Is the organization in a position, emotionally, financially and technically, to implement Cloud Computing?

Chapter 8: What should I ask my vendor?

1. **Is the vendor credible?** Implementing Cloud Computing is a strategic decision; will the vendor be around long enough?

2. **Does the service meet my needs?** Does the service match up with your functional and technical requirements?

3. **How is the service delivered?** The service is probably delivered by a number of suppliers fronted by the vendor you are contracting with. Do you understand the risks associated with every element of the service?

4. **What are the commercial arrangements?** How do you pay for the service, and what flexibility is there in the commercial arrangements?

5. **What legal considerations are there?** When signing up for the service, what are the legal or contractual limitations from the market, regulators or customers?

Throughout the questions we will refer to the "service" which may mean service, software system, software application, software solution or system.

Chapter

Questions for my organization

Self-knowledge is the great power by which we comprehend and control our lives.

Vernon Howard (Philosopher, 1918 – 1992)

C LOUD Computing is simply an umbrella marketing term to describe how software can be provided to your business. Cloud Computing is not an end in itself. Its only purpose is to assist in meeting business goals or addressing businesses challenges or issues. Therefore it is critical that you are clear about what is driving you to consider Cloud Computing and therefore what your needs will be for the Cloud Computing offering. Being clear about this will inform the questions that you ask your vendors.

Let's start with you and your organization.

So get your pencil out as you are bound to want to make notes or at least check off the questions that are relevant to your current situation.

7.1 Why are we considering Cloud Computing?

This section is all about understanding what is motivating you to consider a Cloud Computing solution. After all it is all too easy to get caught up in the hype of the latest "new idea". Be clear about these drivers or goals as they will inform your other questions.

Will Cloud Computing improve your organizations effectiveness and performance? If so, how? Will it give you greater availability of information to your team, wherever they are and whenever they need it? Or improve the mobility of your workforce?

Maybe it is about reducing costs for a commodity service as IT no longer offers you competitive advantage. Or can a 3rd party deliver a better quality service at a lower cost?

Perhaps your existing capabilities are stretched. A recent survey showed that IT departments estimate 83% of their budgets are used to just keep the lights on. That leaves only 17% for new programs. In this environment speculative innovation projects stand little or no chance of funding. This potentially compromises the long term future of new products and services. So Cloud Computing may let you "try before you buy", where someone else has provided the blood for the bleeding edge ideas.

Are your motivations for looking at Cloud Computing offerings driven by a need to reduce or manage business costs? The service does not come from thin air[10]. The point is that there is infrastructure and networks that need to be paid for. True the ability to provide one huge infrastructure and share it across multiple customers will lower the cost for all, but be aware if it is too cheap. Cost reductions targeting the cost of provision may not be the biggest gain. A 10% reduction in the cost of IT may not be as good as a 25% improvement of sales when using slightly more expensive IT. But are there greater benefits to be gained; market expansion, a defensive strategy, or innovation.

Finally, it may enable you to integrate your partners and suppliers in your end to end processes or value chain.

---

[10] In fact it comes from Clouds which are far denser than thin air, which is why aircraft try and fly around Clouds. And if they don't you normally spill your drink!

☒	Question	Why this matters
☐	7.1.1 Are you looking to manage or reduce headcount?	Outsourcing to a Cloud Computing service can reduce the requirement for in-house resources. Some businesses use the outsourcing of services to reduce headcount. Others use it as an opportunity to re-deploy resources to other more valuable roles.
☐	7.1.2 Where are the headcount savings?	The most obvious savings are in IT – development and support. But what business improvement headcount savings are possible? Look more openly across the business for savings.
☐	7.1.3 Are you looking to reduce current infrastructure costs?	The costs savings could include network, hardware, software or maintenance and support. Again you need to be clear about what savings can really be made and which if those can be realized. If infrastructure it is freed up and is reused by a project eliminating new spend then that is a saving. But kit standing idle is not.
☐	7.1.4 How and when will the infrastructure savings occur?	When will the benefits actually accrue? Are the infrastructure cost savings one-off or on-going and are they real cost savings? Do the one-off savings require redeployment of infrastructure? If so, when? Finally, do contracts allow you to reduce or eliminate on-going costs?
☐	7.1.5 Are you looking to avoid new infrastructure expenditure?	New projects or business growth may require additional investment in IT infrastructure within your business. A Cloud Computing solution will provide much of the infrastructure such as servers, security, networking, software etc within the service charge, therefore moving the costs from Capex to Opex

☒	Question	Why this matters
☐	7.1.6 Can you move costs from Capex into long term Opex?	This is viewing IT assets in a similar way to property where few businesses own their property but lease on a long term basis. Could you get a discount for agreeing to a longer term contract and does this improve your business case? For some businesses there may be value in a Capex model and this could open up other avenues for pricing discussions with the Cloud vendor.
☐	7.1.7 Is this an opportunity to drive innovation?	Are there current ways of working which could be changed dramatically with a Cloud Computing approach? Innovation is the driver for future revenue or longer term cost savings. The lack of significant upfront costs allows you to experiment without the traditional "start up costs" for an innovative project
☐	7.1.8 What expansion can you achieve without incurring additional cost?	Will you be able to offer more for less because of the Cloud Computing approach? Are there areas where your expansion is being limited? Are the expansion opportunities geographical, product, operational/support or financial? Will Cloud Computing allow expansion without investment in infrastructure or software, or can you tie the costs to the benefits rather than a large up-front investment?
☐	7.1.9 What geographical expansion is enabled?	Are their sales territories that can now be accessed? Are there regions or time zones that can be supported? Cloud Computing allows you to think far more creatively about both your front and back-office operations.

☒	Question	Why this matters
☐	7.1.10 What R&D is enabled?	Can you be more creative around R&D if your data and operations are enabled by Cloud Computing? Could you access R&D resource outside the organization in other time zones? Could "follow-the-sun" development be a cost-effective possibility?
☐	7.1.11 Do you have peaks in load requiring excess IT capacity?	You may run reports or other processes that require vast number crunching, but only on an ad-hoc basis. Traditional on-premise solutions would require significant infrastructure investment to cope with the ad-hoc requirements, but then remain idle for most of the time. Many Cloud Computing services allow you to run processes on an ad-hoc basis, utilizing the resources you require and paying by consumption.
☐	7.1.12 Are there process improvements you are trying to implement?	Is the Cloud Computing initiative part of a larger business change or improvement exercise? What are the benefits you are trying to achieve? Can you integrate your entire supply chain including partners, suppliers and even customers? Costs for delivering the "integrated" business have traditionally been high due to the complex connectivity and software requirements.
☐	7.1.13 Is this a chance to drive standardized processes?	How consistent are the operations across the business? Are different business units or locations duplicating effort with different tools for the same job /activity? Consistency of operation will make it easier to deploy the service. Is Cloud Computing the opportunity to drive consistency and hence operational efficiency across the organization?

☒	Question	Why this matters
☐	7.1.14 Can you drive an improvement in 'quality' of product or service?	Can you deliver improved design, testing or better support due to Cloud Computing? Can you access overseas resources or employ 'follow-the-sun' techniques. These could improve customer sat, partner sat, or reduce product returns.
☐	7.1.15 Are there opportunities for competitive advantage?	Can you show there will be a gain through: speed to market, enhanced customer sat, partner sat or product or service quality? If you can then you can build a far easier business case. Increased sales are often simpler to demonstrate than reduced costs.
☐	7.1.16 Are there 3rd party savings?	Are you spending money on 3rd parties such as IT contractors which could be reduced or eliminated? Look along the entire supply chain for 3rd parties. In IT there is operations, service delivery, maintenance and upgrades, support, back-up and restore and Disaster Recovery. Some, but not all, could be eliminated. Also look in the business lines where there are often "hidden" resources supporting IT systems.

7.2 What do we need from the service?

In the previous section we looked at the motives for considering Could Computing. Here we look at the questions we need to consider when thinking about the needs or requirements for the service.

Although every project within every company will have specific and differing needs, there will be common threads.

The nature of Cloud Computing i.e. delivered by a 3rd party, over a network, from a remote location which you are not in total control of, means that there are new questions that need to be asked, or questions you would have asked previously, but now need a much tighter focus than when using in-house services e.g. Service Level Agreements.

If you are not happy with an internal service then you can raise the issue up the management chain until it is either rejected or resolved. With 3rd parties involved, resolution will be via good will, change control or ultimately by contract. So you need to consider what you need carefully.

☒	Question	Why this matters
☐	7.2.1 At what times does the service need to be accessed, by region or office?	There may not be a single answer, but it will impact your view on the SLA's for the service and it needs to allow for operations across multiple countries or time zones. Global operations may need a 24 hour, "follow the sun" service, businesses with a warehouse may have overnight operations, and even traditional 9-5 SME businesses may have home workers who will need access during the evening. A salesperson in Australia is not going to appreciate a service that is offline at 2-3am UK time every day.
☐	7.2.2 What are the security policies covering offline data on devices?	Your existing security policies may need to be modified based on the information the service stores on the different devices. You need to be clear about the capabilities of the service and your operational approach and therefore your data strategy to be able to determine the security policies.
☐	7.2.3 What times are mandatory, desirable or simply nice to have?	Can you categorize the needs to understand the cost/benefit of access? You may decide that you need 4 9's (99.99%) availability based on your "ideal" requirements, but how critical is this? There is an exponential cost curve as you go from 2 9's to 4 9's.
☐	7.2.4 From which countries will the service be accessed?	In which countries will the end user need to access the service – not just their home office? Are there different laws, policies or HR legislation by country? Also, what country or region do you consider the mobile workforce to be located for licensing purposes?

☒	Question	Why this matters
☐	7.2.5 What languages need to be supported?	English may be your business language, but what other languages need to be supported? At head office you may believe that English is the core language, but down at an operational level in the regions is that true? And language can be one of the highest barriers to adoption of the new service.
☐	7.2.6 What devices will be used to access the service?	What specific PCs, laptops, browsers and mobile devices do you have in the organization? And what is the exact configuration? This may be a test for your asset management. Do you even know what is out there? PCs and laptops are easier to manage, but what browsers are people using? More challenging is tracking what mobile devices are actually being used? There may be cost implications of procuring or upgrading devices.
☐	7.2.7 What level of security or encryption will be required, by device?	Assume that every device type will be lost or stolen, either by accident or maliciously. What is the business and reputational risk if the data falls into the hands of the competition, organized crime or the press?
☐	7.2.8 Will access be from multiple devices?	How will data synchronization be handled? What are the implications of information on different devices being out of date prior to a sync?

☒	Question	Why this matters
☐	7.2.9 Is access to the information required when not online?	Some of your users may always be connected e.g. office workers. Others such as sales people may not and if they need access even when "off-line" then you will need to consider solutions that offer a hybrid approach with a central "hosted" service and a local synchronized copy.
☐	7.2.10 How critical to the business operation is a lack of online access?	When the connection to the service goes down, what is the implication? You must assume as with any IT service that the connection may go down. This could be for a variety of reasons; your network or outbound connections, your ISP, any part of the internet, vendor internet connection, vendor unplanned maintenance.
☐	7.2.11 What length of time is acceptable for no online access?	How will your business continue to operate and how long before it impacts your ability to work effectively? How long can you live with no access? Do you have an offline copy that you can continue to work with? When the service becomes available how do you sync if only one region has lost connectivity and others are still working live?
☐	7.2.12 Do you need a custom solution or a commodity service?	Is your business really unique or is there a desire to standardize on the operational processes, and hence functionality across regions? Custom solutions are rarely provided as a Cloud Computing service. Cloud Computing is about providing one solution at scale. But what level of local configuration or customization will satisfy the business need?

☒	Question	Why this matters
☐	7.2.13 Do you require different service configurations by region, country, office or department?	How consistent are the operations across the business? Are you planning to perpetuate differing approaches to common processes? Consistency of operation will make it easier to deploy the service. Is Cloud Computing the opportunity to drive consistency and hence operational efficiency across the organization?
☐	7.2.14 What are the internal IT SLAs for the existing service?	What are the expectations for the reliability and availability of any existing services that will be replaced? The higher the SLA's that are included within the service contract the higher the costs. Just because you can ask for 99.999% doesn't mean that you need it. However your motivation to move to a Cloud Computing service may be to significantly enhance the service availability. Ensuring that you have the correct balance between needs and wants is critical.
☐	7.2.15 How often should the data be backed up?	What is the correct frequency for backups? Should your data be backed up every hour, overnight, or weekly? Depending on how quickly your data changes you may need backups more or less frequently. Your data may be sourced from other systems and so can be recreated without backups e.g. a reporting database which extracts data from the transaction database

☒	Question	Why this matters
☐	7.2.16 How quickly do you need access to backups for restore?	If a problem occurs how quickly do you need to be able to access the backup data and restore it? Hopefully the backups are stored off site; however it will therefore take time to get the backup media back. Are other copies retained on-site? If the data is only used as part of overnight processes or for ad-hoc requests, is a longer time frame acceptable?
☐	7.2.17 What Disaster Recovery provision is required?	Although unlikely, it is possible that a catastrophic failure could occur. How quickly do you need the service to be ready to use again? It should be considered whether in-house or a Cloud Computing service. However it is often only reviewed when a 3rd party service is considered. Options range from doing nothing, through, cold, warm, hot and ultimately real time synchronization across multiple locations.
	7.2.18 What are the metrics to measure success?	What are the key metrics? What are the overall end to end process metrics, rather than the Cloud Computing provider metrics?
	7.2.19 How do you measure the Cloud Computing supplier?	What are the key metrics to measure the Cloud Computing provider? It may not be response time, but speed of availability of reports, data transfer or synchronizations.

7.3 What are the internal costs?

With any project there is an obvious and necessary focus on the costs associated with the external vendor, and the Smart Questions that will help you in this area are covered in Chapter 8.

However just as important are the internal costs as it is all too easy for these to be ignored until they end up being the downfall of what originally looked like a "no brainer" project.

These "internal costs to migrate" should be part of any business case; however we often find that with internal projects their importance is overlooked, it will be something that can be addressed later, "After all it's only internal 'funny money' not real out the door costs".

There are also 'internal costs' that get highlighted during the process of understanding the service provided by the vendor. For example we get very serious about the Disaster Recovery process that the vendor provides and yet we often forget about our own internal DR process. Your DR procedures or lack of them may make redundant all the effort you have put in with the vendor.

One often overlooked area is the risk of the multiple "moving parts"; in the end to end process which will include internal procedures, systems and cloud based services from multiple suppliers. This is where internal IT functions tend to play the FUD (fear uncertainty and doubt) card to make it hard to say yes to Cloud Computing when in fact this risk already exists in your existing processes and infrastructure. Particularly as most organizations have poorly defined, maintained and consistently adopted processes.

The costs can take many forms including headcount changes (increases as well as reductions), training, IT upgrades (devices, networks, software), consultants, additional internal processes (some which you should have in place already, but don't!) et al.

☒	Question	Why this matters
☐	7.3.1 What are the costs for guarding against lack of access to the service?	Can you quantify the cost to the business if access to the service is lost? This may be lost income, or delayed time to market, a lower customer service with reputational risks. Understanding the risks and costs associated with a loss of service will enable you to allocate the appropriate solution to mitigate the risks. You may have confidence on the vendor's SLA, but what about your own internet connection, do you need to put in duplicate / redundant connections. Are some risks so costly to fix for the low chance of occurrence that insurance is the appropriate answer.
☐	7.3.2 Have you costed your DR, back-up and restore into the business case?	What are the costs of providing your own capabilities and are they included in your business case? The service provided by the vendor may already include DR and backup, but what about DR and backup in your offices? You need to be very clear about what risks you are mitigating as providing DR, back-up and restore by region can be expensive. Also consider how much of this DR requirement is unique to the project and how much should in fact be standard practice within the business irrespective of this project.

☒	Question	Why this matters
☐	7.3.3 What are the costs of reducing headcount?	The headcount reductions may have a cost associated with them? Have they been quantified? Your HR and procurement teams need to get involved to help you cost the savings and the cost to get the savings. There may be redundancy, relocation or arrangement costs, plus legal bills and internal HR costs. If you were going to get the reductions from natural wastage can you predict the timing?
☐	7.3.4 What are the contractual costs of reducing external headcount?	If you are getting rid of contractors or consultants what contractual terms do you need to abide by in terms of time or penalties? Getting rid of contractors or consultants is never as simple as you first think. They may have termination clauses, minimum notice periods, or have knowledge which needs to be transferred before they go. Sometimes they can cling like barnacles on a rock.
☐	7.3.5 What are the 3rd party costs of reducing headcount?	Are there costs from 3rd parties to remove staff? Are there costs such as legal, recruitment or outplacement which you need to take into account? Or does the company have other policies to reduce internal headcount? Are these factored into the business case?

☒	Question	Why this matters
☐	7.3.6 What costs are there to cover HR claims?	Do you need to provide budget for potential HR claims following the headcount reductions? You should assume that there will be some sort of claim for unfair dismissal even when you have followed a "perfect process". Is there a policy or standard for determining the budget to be allocated? Should this be part of your business case costs?
☐	7.3.7 What are one-off internal costs for setting up the service?	There will be internal effort. How is this costed? Do you need to apply a weighted labor cost? If no resource is available will you need to use a 3rd party? Are you allowed to? If not, and you need to wait for internal resource does this change your migration plans and business case?
☐	7.3.8 What are the one off 3rd party costs??	Do 3rd parties need to support you on the migration? 3rd party costs are a lot less when they are planned in advance. Last minute requests inevitably attract a "you are in trouble and need me now" premium. Have you allowed for these?
☐	7.3.9 What are the costs of upgrading existing IT hardware?	Do you know the costs of all the upgrades for IT equipment (laptops, PCs, mobile)? If the Cloud Computing service requires a specific hardware configuration such as processor, upgraded graphics cards, additional memory or disk space? How long will this take and what internal costs are there?

☒	Question	Why this matters
☐	7.3.10 What are the costs of upgrading software?	Does the current software running support the Cloud Computing service? Does the service require a specific browser, plug-ins or other systems, which you need to procure and install? Do they need to be tested against the existing infrastructure? How long with this take and what internal costs are there?
☐	7.3.11 What network and communications need to be upgraded?	Will you need to upgrade any element of the network or communications to support the increased load? Have you done the capacity planning to ensure that the network will cope with peak loading - in every region? How long will it take to design, test and upgrade, and what internal costs are there?
☐	7.3.12 What integrations with existing systems need to be developed?	What existing systems need to be integrated with the new Cloud Computing service? Rarely are Cloud Computing services completely self contained. At a minimum there are users which are on your current internal domain? How long will these integrations take to develop, or are they out of the box or provided by a 3rd party at additional cost?

☒	Question	Why this matters
☐	7.3.13 What are the costs of data clean up prior to migration?	Have you estimated the costs of cleaning all the data to be converted? The move to a Cloud Computing service may be a great opportunity to clean up existing data. Bad data carried over to the new service can create a poor impression on day one, impacting adoption. One thing is certain, without base data for the users, the acceptance of the service will be a challenge. Has the vendor experience of cleaning data in your format and volumes? Therefore can they estimate accurately or is a 3rd party going to need to be used?
☐	7.3.14 What are the internal costs of data migration?	After cleaning the data, it will need to be migrated and tested. Do you need to include internal costs for this data migration? Your internal IT team will need to export the data and possibly support the migration. Building export/import routines, testing and running migration as just some of the activities.
	7.3.15 How will you physically move your existing data to the new service?	If you have significant data volumes that need to be moved from an existing service to the new one, how will this be moved? Even with a high speed data connection this could take many hours or even days. Do you need to phase the data migration e.g. move users mailboxes in groups every night based on their location or department. Or can you use a tape (or other physical media) to backup your data and then restore at the other location? This can have a significant impact and cost on you migration planning.

☒	Question	Why this matters
☐	7.3.16 What are the 3rd party costs of data migration?	Do you need to include 3rd party costs for this data migration? If your internal IT team are not available or capable of building export/import routines, testing & running migration systems do you need a 3rd party? Are you allowed to use them?
☐	7.3.17 Do the 3rd party resources you use need specialist skills?	Some activities may require specialists with specific certifications or security clearance? Some of your customers may require you to use contractors who are approved to a specified security level (e.g. Governments). Or your insurance or warranties may be invalid if you do not use a "certified" engineer. These types of resources are typically in high demand and you will need to provide longer notice to secure their services.
☐	7.3.18 What DR / roll-back needs to be in place during the migration?	Have you costed the IT infrastructure required to protect the data as it is migrated? The migration is the riskiest time. If the migration fails then what additional capabilities do you need to be able to catch it and roll-back to the previous set-up?
☐	7.3.19 What are the 3rd party costs for training staff?	Is training available, what are the standard costs for training, who provides it and where? For many services they are immature so formal training material hasn't been developed. It is little more than a help file or a few pages on a website. Perhaps the training is only available on-line for the core product. So you need to think about training people on YOUR end to end process, not just the new screens provided by the service

☒	Question	Why this matters
☐	7.3.20 What are the internal costs associated with the training?	Do you need to cost in the time that people spend away from their desks training? If people are on training courses they are not working. Is there a cost, for example, if temp cover needs to be provided? Is unused training budget available?
☐	7.3.21 What is the training cost for 3rd parties?	You may have 3rd parties who have access to your systems, how are you going to train them. Can you mandate that they take the training, and who pays for the training and for their time?
☐	7.3.22 What internal costs for implementation / reengineering?	What are the true costs of implementing – by that we mean reengineering the business processes to take advantage of the Cloud Computing capabilities? Rarely is implementing a Cloud Computing service simply a direct replacement of existing systems. You still need to implement it which means considering the changes to the end to end processes supported by the Cloud Computing service and then configure the service, build integrations to existing systems, train the staff, and conduct a post-implementation review. Whoever said "With Cloud Computing you just turn it on and use it" is a poor liar, a Cloud Computing salesman – or both".

☒	Question	Why this matters
☐	7.3.23 What 3rd party costs for implementation / reengineering?	Do you need to employ a 3rd party consultant to support you? Often the implementation experience is with 3rd party contractors or consulting firms. The Cloud Computing vendor is simply technical. What additional resources are required to deliver the business benefits? Do you need to cost external support and resources such as business analysis, LEAN, Six Sigma, training or IT support? Can you use previous projects to get costing estimates, or do you need to go out and get new estimates?

7.4 What are the external barriers?

Motives understood, needs captured and internal costs identified, so let's go. Hold on there. As highlighted in the short story in Chapter One there may be critical factors outside of your organization that could be a barrier to success.

What are the possible external barriers that could prevent you moving to Cloud Computing? What legislation applies to your industry or has been imposed by customers? Are there geopolitical factors that need to be considered, would your US office be happy with you using a datacenter in North Korea even if all legal requirements were satisfied?

As the market for Cloud Computing matures so the expectations and requirements upon you or your customers, partners or other 3rd parties matures. It is increasingly common to see contracts or tender documents with requirements for recognized standards in security (ISO27001) or service management (ITIL), do these apply to you or your customers. How will the fact that Cloud Computing means that your data has escaped your corporate data center affect you?

☒	Question	Why this matters
☐	7.4.1 Can access to the service be provided in all locations?	Access to the service will require an internet connection. Different locations or devices may have specific requirements. If your offices are in major urban areas then internet connectivity may not be an issue. However offices in remote or rural locations may not have the same low cost access and may require more expensive solutions. Is your asset management and configuration control good enough to manage this, consistently?
☐	7.4.2 What data management obligations do you have?	What laws, regulations, policies and standards do you need to be aware of, in each country in which you operate? Are these driven by regulatory bodies or customer needs? Although internally a business may be relaxed about who can see what, there are often clear legal requirements for retention and privacy and these may vary depending on the countries you operate in.
☐	7.4.3 What data needs to be stored as part of the service?	What security classification is the data? Is it internal or customer data? The classification of the data will impact the costs of security, back-up and storage. It may even make using Cloud Computing unworkable.

☒	Question	Why this matters
☐	7.4.4 Where will the datacenters storing your data be?	The nature of Cloud Computing means that the vendor is managing your data for you and will want to optimize costs by making efficient use of resources. This may mean using datacenters outside your country. The rights of the local authorities to access 3rd party data in their jurisdiction vary significantly, however you should assume that if required they can access your data. Therefore you need to consider whether data needs to be held in specific locations to maximize your chances of protecting it. Some countries have put laws in place to ensure the security of national data and these may determine where data can be held.
☐	7.4.5 Have your customers specified requirements for the location of data storage	Organizations are becoming increasingly aware of the requirements for protecting data where it is held by 3rd parties and are including these requirements in contract terms. Where you store data on behalf of or about customers you will have an implied or possibly explicit responsibility for its security. Even if the customer is not currently aware of this situation you can be sure they will raise it if something goes wrong. Consider US data in North Korea, or Iranian data held in a US data center.

☒	Question	Why this matters
☐	7.4.6 Do your customers require clear segregation of their data?	Customers may wish to be satisfied that there data is clearly isolated from other customers data. To achieve the economies of scale in Cloud Computing the physical infrastructure is normally shared, not just across your data, but across other customers of the vendor. To offer physical as well as logical segregation increases the costs of the service and may require greater testing and procedural effort.
☐	7.4.7 Does the DR service offered meet regulatory requirements?	Are there different levels of DR (Disaster Recovery) required for market, risk, legal or regulatory reasons for each region? Have you assessed the risks of each location to determine the correct level of DR? Are they driven by market, physical or regulatory factors?
☐	7.4.8 Does the back-up and restore service offered meet regulatory requirements?	Are there different levels of back-up and restore required for each region? Have you assessed the risks of each location to determine the correct level of back-up and restore? Are they driven by market, physical or regulatory factors?
☐	7.4.9 Does the service meet your customer commitment for DR?	What commitments have you made to you customers about DR for their data? Are they contractual commitments or softer 'expectations' or worse, implied commitments. What was put in your proposal to the customer which you used to win the work?

☒	Question	Why this matters
☐	7.4.10 Does the service meet your customer commitment for back-up and restore?	What commitments have you made to you customers about back-up and restore for their data? Are they contractual commitments or softer 'expectations' or worse, implied commitments? What was put in your proposal to the customer which you used to win the work?
☐	7.4.11 Can the DR be proven for customer audits and at what cost?	Can customers audit you on your DR arrangements? Can you even visit and demonstrate your DR capabilities? Are there costs associated with letting your customers view the DR capability – by the Cloud Computing vendor or travel costs if abroad? How often and to what extent are you expected to carry out DR rehearsals?
☐	7.4.12 Can the back-up and restore be proven for customer audits and at what cost?	Can customers audit you on your back-up and restore arrangements? Can you even visit and demonstrate your back-up and restore capabilities? Are there costs associated with letting your customers view the back-up and restore capability – by the Cloud Computing vendor or travel costs if abroad? How often and to what extent are you expected to carry out data restore rehearsals? Backups are only valuable if they can be restored!!!

☒	Question	Why this matters
☐	7.4.13 Are there required formats for data backups?	Has the customer specified a specific format that their data must be stored in as part of a backup? Some organizations are concerned about the use of proprietary formats as they may be unable to read their own data at a later date without access to the proprietary tools. They are therefore specifying "open" or human readable formats such as XML.
☐	7.4.14 What are your contractual commitments for existing services?	If you are providing customers or partners with access to information are there SLAs or other contractual terms? Would changes in the SLAs, contractual commitments or softer 'expectations' or worse, implied commitments leave you exposed to litigation? What was put in the proposal which you used to win the work?
☐	7.4.15 Will any customer or 3rd party contracts need to be renegotiated?	If the SLAs or other terms are materially changed are there customer contracts that need to be renegotiated? Are there risks in renegotiating contracts with customers, as it forces them to look at the costs and benefits of your offering? But if you fail to raise the changes are you at greater risk of litigation?
☐	7.4.16 Can you back-to-back the commitment to customers to your contracts with the vendor?	Are you able to tie customer commitments to the SLAs provided by the Cloud Computing vendor? You can reduce your exposure with a back to back contract, but it does not get you off the hook.

☒	Question	Why this matters
☐	7.4.17 What 3rd parties will require access?	Do you need to give 3rd parties such as partners, outsourcers or contractors access? Who is picking up the costs? Are the technical, procedural and legal issues the same as for an employee?

7.5 Are we ready internally?

One of the single largest factors determining whether a project will be successful or not is whether the organization is ready internally. This is not just about Cloud Computing or even IT projects. Every project where there is any degree of change will be successful based on the adoption of the change by the workforce[11].

Projects that have clear executive sponsorship and a well defined business case that is accepted by the key stakeholders are off to a flying start. However the management of change within the business and the support required by the users of the new system is critical. Finally it is about 'adoption'. If the new system, application, way of working, approach or whatever is not accepted and adopted by the end users, then the benefits will never be delivered.

It is also important that there is recognition of the organizations "style". It is rarely a good idea to try and push through a high risk, bleeding edge idea with nothing more than a promise and a prayer. There is even less chance in organizations that are highly risk averse either by tradition or due to the environment they operate in. By understanding these factors you can ensure that you have addressed the needs of the organization as part of the project.

Have you made sure that the business case is realistic and covers not just the obvious, but the more subtle aspects of the project? You can be sure that someone will ask, and even if they don't raise it in advance they certainly will if the project goes tits-up[12].

Have you considered whether this projects links into other projects or a wider program of change within the business. Getting this right can be the difference between being perceived as stepping on other people toes and/or gaining key supporters in other parts of the business.

---

[11] In fact, my first book covered just this point. A summary is in the Appendix

[12] An important project management term. Similar to FUBAR!

☒	Question	Why this matters
☐	7.5.1 Is the business ready for change, by location?	Have you conducted a business readiness survey for each impacted location? If certain groups have other priorities or they are resistant to change then does the business case still stack up?
☐	7.5.2 Are the benefits sufficient to make the changes happen?	Are there sufficient incentives to make the changes? Change normally requires a significant catalyst to get going and enough of a return to get it to continue. Without the correct incentives projects can easily be sidelined and die a slow death.
☐	7.5.3 Is there enough 'political will'?	Are members of senior management aligned to the changes? Are you burning your personal political capital to get the project going? Would it be better to get wider support before you get going?
☐	7.5.4 Do you have an Executive Sponsor?	Do you have an Executive Sponsor and do they really understand the business case? An Executive Sponsor is often difficult to get for any program of change. But good Executive Sponsorship is even rarer. A true test of support is whether they will publically defend the business case? If not why not? This is true for all projects, however the "new" nature of Cloud Computing projects may increase the board's risk awareness and makes sponsorship even more important.

☒	Question	Why this matters
☐	7.5.5 Does your Executive Sponsor understand Cloud Computing?	Does your Executive Sponsor understand the implications of Cloud Computing on your business? What training, education do you need arrange to get your Executive Sponsor up to speed? Do you need to find someone else? Without understanding how will they be able to support the project when the going gets tough (which it does on all projects!!)?
☐	7.5.6 How change-averse is the organization?	If the benefits require a change in working practices in different areas of the business, is there a history of inertia? A business case built on process improvements in an organization which is reluctant to change is weak. What catalyst will change that behavior? Competition, change of leadership, customer pressure.
☐	7.5.7 Does the organization have a block on 3rd party services?	Is Cloud Computing seen as a 3rd party service and therefore subject to a procurement block? Some organizations are putting blanket blocks on all 3rd party spend or outsourcing. Are there contracting limitations which say that all outsourcing needs to be provided or offered through a single vendor? Do you need to be careful how you categorize the Cloud Computing service?

☒	Question	Why this matters
☐	7.5.8 Does this project support a wider change program?	You have a series of change programs which are themselves delivering benefits. Does Cloud Computing support or change them? Your business case may not have taken into account the reduction in value because of the impact on existing programs or maybe Cloud Computing enhances their value. Programs that are in-flight may be difficult to change. This may impact your ability to even implement Cloud Computing.
☐	7.5.9 What risks are there with the migration?	Have you identified the potential points of failure? The greatest risk is during the migration. What can go wrong, probably will. Planning for the disasters will mitigate many of the risks.
☐	7.5.10 Is parallel running required and has it been costed into the business case?	Is the migration and service such high risk that a level of parallel running (new and existing system) required? This is extremely expensive in terms of staff and computing resource. But it may be necessary. If so, it needs to be planned and costed.
☐	7.5.11 Have you planned the roll-back if parallel running fails?	Is the implementation such high risk that you need parallel running? Whilst parallel running sounds safer, have you planned the criteria for reverting back and the implications in terms of business disruption, costs, and your reputation? And once you have rolled back, then what?

☒	Question	Why this matters
☐	7.5.12 Is there an internal innovation budget?	Do you have budgets ring-fenced around innovation or innovative-related activities? Can you fund the Cloud Computing project from this budget? Or at a minimum can you consider Cloud Computing to be innovative so that you can fund a pilot?
☐	7.5.13 If the Capex budget is not spent will it be lost?	Does your company have a "spend it or lose it" budgeting approach? If you do not spend from the Capex budget will it roll-over so it is available next year? Or will your budget be cut for next year because you didn't spend it? Even though Cloud Computing is usually paid as Opex, you may be able to use Capex that would otherwise be lost to cover an initial period.
☐	7.5.14 What internal data management policies need to be adhered to?	What internal security policies do you have and do they cater for the Cloud Computing paradigm? Often these policies were crafted when all data sat on a computer that was managed "in house" and do not reflect the differences of the Cloud Computing approach. Also consider how they may need to vary by location to reflect local legal requirements.
☐	7.5.15 How can you satisfy Data Protection requirements, by country?	What Data Protection requirements do you need to satisfy, in each country in which you operate? The laws are different by country. And you need to consider if there are different requirements when the data sits on a Cloud Computing platform.

☒	Question	Why this matters
☐	7.5.16 What time in the financial year or business cycle is best for the migration?	Are there periods of time where change is impossible or more likely to fail? Change is never easy so you need to pick the optimum time so that you get maximum attention. This may be determined by other initiatives or market seasonality.
☐	7.5.17 Is the migration big bang or phased by country, region or department?	Have you thought through the implications of big bang vs. a phased approach? Big bang is clearly higher risk, however with a phased approach there may be issues with data duplication or increased costs in migration. Can you clearly separate one phase from the next?
☐	7.5.18 Are there other project dependencies?	Do you require other projects or activities to be in place first? These may be change programs, organizational changes, new systems or upgrades, market changes, customer contracts or legislative changes.
☐	7.5.19 Do you have mechanisms in place to track SLAs?	Can you measure the SLAs that the vendor is meeting? If you are going to claim service credits (discounts/refunds) if the vendor does not meet their SLAs then you will need to be able to monitor and record them. Don't rely on the vendor owning up.

☒	Question	Why this matters
☐	7.5.20 Are your financial models suited to assessing Cloud Computing offerings?	Has the company experience of building a business case for a Cloud Computing service with monthly charge and no upfront costs? Discounted Cash Flow analysis works well for traditional on-premise projects, where there is often a substantial first year cost and only a running cost going forward. If your models do not reflect the costs appropriately then you may find that no matter how logical the savings are, you will struggle to move the project through the review and approval stages. This may require upfront work to agree a revised business case model. It has been known for businesses to request an alternate "all in year one" cost to help fit the costs to the model.
☐	7.5.21 Are your financial models capable of assessing the risks?	Do you understand how to quantify the risk of a Cloud Computing service and reflect it in the financial model? Transferring the risk to a Cloud Computing vendor may actually increase the organization's risk. How is this reflected in the financial model?
☐	7.5.22 Do your financial models enable you to assess the value of the different charging approaches?	Is there any value given to not investing up front - i.e. 'Cost of Cash'? There is a value in not investing up front in software and infrastructure, as you would for an on-premise or in-house project. But is this in the financial model? Do the financial models support the charging approaches offered by the vendor?

☒	Question	Why this matters
☐	7.5.23 What are the accounting policies, by region?	Do you have any policies for accounting for Cloud Computing? Do you understand how they vary by region? There are many different Cloud Computing charging models. Do you have in place the accounting policies, or access to the audit advice on how to account for these costs? These accounting approaches may and will vary by region.
☐	7.5.24 Do you auditors have relevant experience of Could Computing, by region?	Have your auditors got real experience of applying Cloud Computing? By real experience we mean they have been challenged by the tax authorities and defended their case. Simply giving some advice based on their interpretation of the Cloud Computing model is not good enough.
☐	7.5.25 Are their tax breaks or accounting benefits, by region?	Cloud Computing may benefit for some form of tax benefit in some regions. The tax benefits may be for innovation or developing IP. Creating the "digital economy" is a key initiative for many Governments, can you benefit from this?
☐	7.5.26 What budgets need to be increased for set up, migration and implementation?	Cloud Computing changes the flow and timing of investment, so has this been reflected into budgets? Budgets that were Capex based with a focus on year one spend, may need to be altered to allow the funds to be spent over multiple years.

☒	Question	Why this matters
☐	7.5.27 What budgets need to be revised for the on-going costs over next 3-5 years?	Cloud Computing changes the flow and timing of investment, so has this been reflected into budgets? The ongoing costs of the service need to be in someone's budget. Is it IT, or is it allocated to the business area consuming the service? Some organizations have strict "one year at a time budgets". What happens if you are signing up for a service where monthly payments are due in the next budget year? You have to make a commercial commitment but with no guarantee of funding!
☐	7.5.28 Does this project impact the scope or ROI of current programs or initiatives?	If you implement Cloud Computing how will this impact the scope or ROI of existing change programs? Will this hinder or help them? This may change your ROI or even prevent you implementing your project. Will Cloud Computing change the benefit profile for other programs? Will this make their ROI invalid? Is the net effect positive or negative – now and for the future?
☐	7.5.29 Do you have a plan to realize the benefits?	If you are reducing 3rd party costs this is usually easy, however headcount reduction or re-training requires planning. Process improvement will typically require some form of change program, which again needs to be planned. The lack of a clear plan to capture the defined benefits for a project is one of the major reasons for the financial failure of projects. Technology in itself is never the answer; it is the extent to which it is integrated into, adopted by and supportive of the business.

☒	Question	Why this matters
	7.5.30 What is the benefits profile?	How do you deliver the benefits? It could be one of 4 profiles. 1. Whoosh and maintain, 2. One off 3. Incremental and slow build over time 4. Immediate and slow decline
☐	7.5.31 Is the ROI hard cash or intangible benefits and are they defensible?	Can you justify and support the claims for the benefits in the business case? When put under pressure can you support your business case and benefits? Whilst the business case shows benefits, are there other factors that mean the benefits may not be realized. That does not necessarily mean the project should not go ahead. Such factors include; the company is constantly in change, political reasons why headcount reductions will not be made or other programs will subsume yours before the benefits are delivered.
☐	7.5.32 Where are the sensitivities in the ROI case?	What elements of your business case, if they change, will blow your business case – or make it much better? If you don't understand the sensitivities then you cannot be sure that the benefits will accrue as the business changes throughout the program.
☐	7.5.33 Is there a specific innovation ROI calculation?	Is there a standard approach for accounting for innovation benefits? Innovation is often hard to quantify and therefore is discounted in any ROI calculations.

☒	Question	Why this matters
☐	7.5.34 Are the costs in the business case already in other budgets?	Are there other budgets that you can raid for the Cloud Computing project? A project to fix a quality issue probably has quite a lot of fat built into the budgets. Can you separate out parts of your project so they can utilize other budgets e.g. training?
☐	7.5.35 What bandwidth will you need at peak, by location?	Have you understood the bandwidth requirements both internally and across the firewall by location? If you work in a large company today, you may have noticed that around lunch time access to the internet slows down. Why? Because lots of people are browsing the internet while they are having a sandwich! Internal "wired" networks typically move data at speeds between 10M and 1G+. Your internet connection is likely to be in the 1-10M range. If all your users are now accessing the internet, will this be enough? Most Cloud Computing offerings today have a low "bandwidth" requirement but it is worth checking. You may need to enhance your connections from the office to the internet. The vendor may be able to provide a usage or sizing guide, but factor in your own testing to validate these claims.

☒	Question	Why this matters
☐	7.5.36 If you need greater bandwidth how long will it take to put the capability in place, by location?	If after testing it is clear you need additional capacity for the connection to the internet, you will have to contact your service providers and request changes and this will take time. This may be more than just an additional line or two. Does it require new routers, new pipes or even a new exchange? This could be a major infrastructure project which takes time to put in place. You may have to renegotiate contracts with your network suppliers.
☐	7.5.37 What Disaster Recovery do you need to put in place internally and how long will it take?	Your Cloud Computing provider may offer DR for their applications and data, but you have your own infrastructure that may need DR. It is pointless demanding and paying for the highest levels of redundancy and disaster recovery from your service provider only to leave your internal systems as the major point of weakness.
☐	7.5.38 What devices do you need to provide?	Do you understand what the specification is for devices that you need to access the service? The 'minimum specification' that the vendor quotes to access the service may not deliver a user experience that is acceptable.
☐	7.5.39 Do existing devices need to be upgraded?	Do you have sufficient asset information to understand what devices need to be upgraded across your organization? You need to consider operating system, memory, storage, additional software systems required to access the service, and possible conflicts with existing systems.

☒	Question	Why this matters
☐	7.5.40 Do you need to swap out / standardize on mobile devices?	If you are accessing the service with mobile devices are there a sub-set of devices you will make standard? Choice of mobile device seems to be very emotive with every person wanting their personal choice. But supporting a massive range of devices can be a nightmare. And this problem is made worse if mobiles are provided by the employee not the company.
☐	7.5.41 Do you have a clear training plan for all staff that will "touch" the new service?	As well as the end users there may be many different skills required to maximize the use of the service and they will all need training. Although one of the big pluses of Cloud Computing is that it reduces the setup and installation efforts, this does not remove the need to train users. In fact it is a great opportunity to use some of the "saved costs" to train the users and supporting staff (business analysts, developers who can integrate to other business systems et al) more effectively to maximize the adoption and success of the service.

Chapter 8

What should I ask my vendor?

Caveat Emptor – a principle in commerce:; without a warranty the buyer takes the risk.

Latin phrase translated to "Let the buyer beware"

C LOUD Computing is an evolving market and although there are an increasing number of corporate vendors, there are still many who are small, entrepreneur driven companies. As always there are pros and cons for different vendor types, the key is to understand what type you are dealing with.

Government at risk

An example of this was the IT Director of a major Government Department. When performing a QA for a project integrating two key customer systems, it was identified that they were using a small piece of 'bridge' software which was critical to the integration. When asked about the software, no-one seemed to know much about the company providing it. So they phoned the number on the website. It was answered by a middle-aged woman who openly admitted she knew nothing about software. When asked for one of the Directors of the company by name she said "Oh. He went out with his brother last night. He probably got drunk as he hasn't come home yet. And it was 11am. So she was casually asked how old he was. He's 18 and his brother is 20, and yes they did write computer programs up in their bedroom, she confirmed. Panic stations and red faces all around the Department.

Quickly they purchased the source code and got a team up to speed on the code. Fortunately it was written in a language which was a standard for the Department.

So, what if they had never asked those questions?

Despite the above story small is not necessarily bad, just as big is not always good. This is all about understanding the risks and understanding the vendor will help determine how far you dig.

You may be horrified with the idea, but you are probably already using Cloud Computing in various parts of the business – well under the radar and a long way from the control and due diligence of your IT department.

Perhaps now is the time for an amnesty. Get the business to come clean and declare what they are doing. Then you can perform a risk assessment using these questions, and get the business back under control, without losing the benefits.

Cloud Computing enables some small and highly innovative vendors to provide a great service. And deliver it far more quickly and far cheaper than a larger vendor and certainly quicker than the in-house team. And this is not necessarily because they have cut corners or made compromises on quality.

"Under the radar" sales and marketing are a key go-to-market strategy for innovative products and services. A Cloud Computing model is perfect to prove a new concept, to jump start a new area, or to drive transformational change. The problem comes when they become strategic by default, with no thought about the implications or due diligence.

These questions should prompt you to stop and thinking clearly about what you are committing the business to long term. You could even use the questions as the basis of your vendor ITT.

8.1 Is the vendor credible?

You are going to be dependent on your vendor every hour of every day. So are they going to be around tomorrow, next year and for the foreseeable future? In a world which is changing rapidly, where even long established global investment banks disappear overnight, then we can have no long term certainty. But we need to make sure that we have asked the Smart Questions and assessed the risks.

Please note that although we indicate in a number of the following questions to ask for "3 years" information, this may not be possible. Many of the Cloud Computing providers have not been around for 3 years and they may also have limited customer lists. This does not make them bad and in fact it may be possible to argue that more established vendors who do not have a Cloud Computing service for a market that is demanding one could be a larger risk. However you do need to understand the risks of working with startups and plan accordingly.

☒	Question	Why this matters
☐	8.1.1 What are the vision and mission, of the vendor?	What is it they do – in a succinct sentence? It will describe their intent and hint at future direction? There is a huge amount of hype around Cloud Computing and it would be good to understand that there is a well thought out plan and vision for the companies foray into this new world. Many Cloud Computing companies are startups (i.e. less than 3 years old) and have not reached adolescence, let alone responsible adulthood. So you want to see a little maturity that gives you the confidence to sign up to a 3 year agreement and trust them with your data. Is there adult supervision on the premises?!
☐	8.1.2 What is the long term goal?	What is the long term goal of the vendor, management team, investors, and are they aligned? Is their ambition matched by their ability and resources? Often difficult to get an honest answer to this question. But the key here is to understand if there is realism to the ambitions? And do they have the "extended" team aligned and behind them?
☐	8.1.3 Are there solid investors and shareholders?	Do you know who is backing the company and what support, incentive and influence they have? An early stage company will need deep pockets or a supportive backer until monthly recurring revenue builds. Critically for you, will they stay in business? Even for more established businesses the changes from upfront to recurring revenue streams may require short term funding to cover the changeover.

☒	Question	Why this matters
☐	8.1.4 What is the track record of the investors?	If the investors have a large or controlling interest, what is their track record? Is it steady investment and growth, or build and flick? Whilst the investors don't drive the company, if they have a large stake they will strongly influence strategy. Being sold to a larger company may be the right answer for a Cloud Computing company's customers as it may give stability.
☐	8.1.5 Do they have the experience of growth?	Is the company going to require a complete change of management in the next 3 years as it grows? What experience has the management team of growing a multi-national organization? Cloud Computing has the potential to grow very rapidly, with the inevitable growing pains. Will the company need 'adult supervision' within a couple of years? Any change of this nature will potentially defocus the company or require significant additional funding.
☐	8.1.6 What are the vendor internal barriers to expansion?	What will stop the company growing? Politics? Funding? Key skills missing? Are there available skills to support the growth? Partnering rather than hiring staff will be a key competence for Cloud Computing companies. Do they have the skills and correct attitude to partnering? Is there sufficient funding to support their growth ambitions? Do they have the product expertise, or support from their core platform vendor i.e. Microsoft? Or are they using unproven products that won't necessarily scale?

☒	Question	Why this matters
☐	8.1.7 How many employees?	How many employees in the company by location, by year for the last 3 years? Get the number of employees broken down by location and employment status (employed, temp, associates) and their role (sales, professional services, development, support). Get ready for a shock: "impressive product + cool website" does not equal a large full-time workforce.
☐	8.1.8 How many related 3rd parties?	Who are the partnerships / JV / 3rd parties that support the delivery of the service? The company you are contracting with may be small (by various measures) and this may raise concerns. However they may be working with Tier 1 partners and this may reduce the risks. They may be using a major hosting provider, who can step in to continue the service. They may have the backing of a strategic industry supplier e.g. Microsoft who are providing support to ensure the services success. Look behind the scenes to see how your risks might be reduced.
☐	8.1.9 Reference customers?	Who are the reference customers and how similar is their use of the service to your requirements? They may be a similar company, but their use of the service may be very different. How mature is their use of the service? Are they still in the honeymoon period which is at least 6 months? Critically, have they been in live operation longer than a release cycle i.e. have they dealt with a new release when running live?

☒	Question	Why this matters
☐	8.1.10 3rd party validation?	Is there 3rd party validation or assessment of the service? If there is a 3rd party assessment, how relevant, independent and current is it? Often analysts will be paid by vendors to write assessments. What? Really? Cloud Computing is all about incremental increases in functionality, so how valid are the comments if the service has evolved since the report? Search online for people's comments about the service, but also remember that people are always quicker to complain than to praise.
☐	8.1.11 Financial results for last 3 years and forecasts?	What were the audited revenue, costs and profits for last 3 years and forecasts for next 3 years? If there aren't audited financial results, why not? What are the sensitivities on the forecasts?
☐	8.1.12 What are their banking facilities?	Who are the primary bankers in each region and what lending facilities are in place? It is not unusual for an early stage, or even late stage, Cloud Computing vendor to be maxed out on credit whilst they wait for revenue to build but are forced to invest. Critically for you, will they stay in business?
☐	8.1.13 What is their asset to liability ratio?	How solvent is the company in terms of their assets vs. liabilities How long will they continue to be able to stay in business?
☐	8.1.14 Balance sheet strength?	How much cash do they have? What is their run or burn rate? Simple question. How long will they continue to be able to stay in business if they took no new orders?

☒	Question	Why this matters
☐	8.1.15 Number of debtor days?	What is their spread of risk? Are they struggling to collect? Average debtor days greater than 50 suggests that something is wrong. Cash collection should be easy for a service where you switch it off if the customer is not paying. If not, are there other issues such as the service has problems, is not sticky or they have poor back office operation.
☐	8.1.16 Level of customer churn?	What is the period of time that customers stay on the service? Do customers migrate off before the contract is due for renewal? Is the churn masked by the company's growth? Often Cloud Computing is adopted by one small area of a major corporation. Once central IT finds out the project is restricted or stopped. Often the initial sign-up is a 12 month contract so the churn figures are hidden. They should have usage patterns so you can see the real value or stickiness or the service.
☐	8.1.17 Span of support?	How many countries are currently supported, and from which locations Who is providing the support - full time staff, associates, resellers, 3rd parties? Or all from one location running 3 shifts. When you call you want to be sure there is someone there.

☒	Question	Why this matters
☐	8.1.18 Helpdesk support hours and languages?	What are the support hours and which languages are supported across those hours? Saying you support French when you have one French speaker with a 24 x 7 business is stretching it a bit. Ask if you can carry out blind testing of the helpdesk before you sign up. This may require a "dummy" customer code, but if the service provider is confident in their support team then there should be no objection.
☐	8.1.19 Professional services and materials across the regions?	What locations are their professional services staff, and which languages do they speak? Although the core service will be in the Cloud, you may wish to provide integration with existing on-premise solutions and therefore require on-site assistance. Claiming that you can deliver consulting in Swedish with one token Dane who can 'get by in Swedish' does not count. Do they have an implementation methodology?
☐	8.1.20 SLA track performance, over the last 3 years?	Do they even have a 3 year track record? If so, is it with the same data center? Can they list the outages and routine maintenance downtime? This is all about understanding the risks. Small is not necessarily bad, just as big is not always good. Understanding the vendor's track record will help determine how far you dig.

☒	Question	Why this matters
☐	8.1.21 Successful customer migrations, over the last 3 years?	How many customers are happy to claim that their migration was a success and are they of a similar size and complexity? Can you talk to them? A successful migration of many small businesses may be a good sign, but does it reflect the different needs of your enterprise scale business with multiple locations and requirements for back office integration (and vice versa). However being first can have its advantages as you will be able to ensure lots of attention from the vendor (assuming you have asked for it!)
☐	8.1.22 Is there an active User Group?	Is there an active independent User Group? The key words here are 'Independent' and 'Active'. How often do they meet? What is their agenda? Who are active members?
☐	8.1.23 What is the size of the user group membership?	How many customers are members, by region? A user group with no members is not very helpful. But a new user group could allow you to be a founding member and increase your influence. Is there a single international User Group? This could mean international travel to get to meetings; however this could introduce you to users from other regions that can highlight requirements as you expand into the other geographies.
☐	8.1.24 What are the User Group agendas?	What were the agenda items for the last 3 meetings? Are they customer or company presentations? This should give you some insights into the maturity of the product, the scale and breadth of the customer base.

☒	Question	Why this matters
☐	8.1.25 Attendance for meetings?	Who attended for the last 3 User Group meetings? This shows a level of support for the product, and hence the chance of long term survival of the vendor.

8.2 Does the service meet my needs?

So it's a simple question. Hopefully you have spent time and effort defining what you want from the service. Now you need to make sure the service meets your needs. If not how much does it matter?

Have you developed a rigorous list and actually seen how the service supports each requirement on the list? Have you weighted the importance of the functionality so you can assess the impact of 'does not meet' items? Describing the functions in terms of end to end processes is really effective and far better than the 'wish-list' approach.

☒	Question	Why this matters
☐	8.2.1 Is the service a decrease in current functionality?	Will the service be a perceived reduction in functionality for users? If you are reengineering the operation this may not be an issue as there will be changes and less may be seen as more. But if the new service is simply replacing an in-house solution how will you deal with end user workarounds and dissatisfaction?
☐	8.2.2 Is the service DR, backup and restore acceptable?	What level of DR, back-up and restore do you need? How much of this do you want to rely on the vendor, or should you provide this yourself? Although this is often overlooked for internal projects, it is even more critical for a service provided by a 3rd party that you understand how the service is protected and managed in the event of a disaster.
☐	8.2.3 Is the service multi-tenant?	Is the service multi-tenanted, and does it matter to you? Multi-tenanted has benefits for the Cloud Computing vendor; one instance of software to update and critically a very low cost to acquire new customers. For you there are downsides; forced to take upgrades, another customer takes the service down or kills performance and potential security breaches.

☒	Question	Why this matters
☐	8.2.4 Are there "size" limitations?	Does unlimited mean unlimited? Or is there a tiered pricing where you get hooked on a limited functionality, limited data volume model and then need to take the premium services? Be very clear on what are the limitations of each of the service offerings. Are there database limitations, limits to the number of records, number of users, number of objects, access to functionality, nag messages, obtrusive Cloud Computing vendor branding etc etc.
☐	8.2.5 Level of organizational complexity supported?	Is the service geared up for your organization in terms of regions, countries, departments, SKU, pay grades? Many of these issues are fundamental in terms of the data structure of the underlying service. They cannot be changed, and any workarounds will rapidly become tiresome.

☒	Question	Why this matters
☐	8.2.6 Languages supported and localization?	What languages are supported for the screens, help, training and supporting information? Can any of this be tailored for local terminology? What languages do you work in now, and in the next 5 years? How prepared are users to access a service using generic terms which could be unfamiliar? Does the service support non-Latin languages; Chinese, Japanese or Arabic? Also can one user see the service in their language and another in their language – including mix of Latin and non-Latin? A huge barrier to adoption and a risk to implementation is to provide a service where staff are using a non-native language.
☐	8.2.7 How is single sign-on supported?	How does it support log-on for the entire organization. Are there integration points so you can use an existing Active Directory or LDAP source for single sign on? Whilst logging on again, does not seem to be a big issue it is often a huge barrier to use. Getting single sign-on to work can be a difficult technical issue for IT departments.

☒	Question	Why this matters
☐	8.2.8 Minimum supported spec, by device?	What is the minimum supported spec, by device to give you the performance and capability that you need? Often the minimum specification is the 'barely workable' set up. You may not be able to access certain functions, have an acceptable performance. Check with other existing customers with similar needs.
☐	8.2.9 What browsers are supported, by device	What browser version is required, but also what plug-ins or add-on software is required. Is the browser version different by device? Do you even know whether you need to upgrade? Do you have sufficient information about the devices deployed across your organization? What about employees accessing the service from home? Your organization may have strict controls that "lock down" a desktop setup and restrict the use of certain plug-ins e.g. ActiveX. To create exceptions may take time (assuming it is possible).

☒	Question	Why this matters
☐	8.2.10 What 3rd party add-ons are required?	Are there 3rd party add-ons which enable you to meet the requirements? This is a two edged sword. On the one hand a rich "ecosystem" of 3rd parties offers extra services to the core product. However adding 3rd party products increases the risks by spreading the number of vendors you need to deliver the service. The questions you've just asked about the Cloud Computing vendor may now need to be asked of all the 3rd party vendors.
☐	8.2.11 Can the service be customized or configured?	Can the service be customized, by your organization, by device? Customization sounds great, but there are implications. Be very careful. Firstly, it is unlikely you can change the core code and certainly not without breaking warranties. Secondly, if you can make changes, how do new releases of the core product affect the changes you have made? Configuration is about making changes that do not affect the core service and therefore upgrades. However a heavily configured service means that you cannot use the standard training. Secondly configuration is a slippery slope with end users demands pushing you into customization. Aim for using the functionality as intended.

☒	Question	Why this matters
☐	8.2.12 Are there tools to configure or customize?	To be able to tweak the service you need the development and testing tools. Are they provided and how good are they? If you are customizing or configuring a service then you need to be able to do it quickly and easily. You may want to make changes once the service has gone live. When the changes have been made can you test them in a 'sandbox' before applying them to the live service?
☐	8.2.13 Are there 3rd party tools to configure or customize?	Do you need to use 3rd party tools because core service tools are not good enough or not available? Adding 3rd party products increases the risks. The questions you've just asked about the Cloud Computing vendor may need to be asked of all the 3rd party vendors.
☐	8.2.14 What integration with 3rd party products or services is available?	Are integrations with 3rd party products available and how are they certified by the supplier? You have legacy systems that are run in-house. Rarely is the Cloud Computing service an island of automation. How are you going to integrate the service to existing systems? This is normally the greatest barrier to a seamless user experience; multiple sign-ons, exports and imports, workarounds.

☒	Question	Why this matters
☐	8.2.15 What 3rd party integrations are on the roadmap?	Although this may provide comfort be aware that this is betting on futures. Anything in the roadmap may not happen. If this capability is a high priority requirement, how far can you push the vendor to "guarantee" its delivery? You may end up having to pay extra for this comfort.
☐	8.2.16 What tools to build integrations?	What tools are provided to build integrations? Simple integrations could be built, but are these only structured export and import routines? What integration tools are offered by 3rd parties? However remember that adding 3rd party products increases the risks. The questions you've just asked about the Cloud Computing vendor may need to be asked of all the 3rd party vendors.
☐	8.2.17 On-line vs. offline functionality?	What functionality is available on-line vs. offline, by different device or service? Despite the hype, not every user is always connected. In the next 5 years it may be true. But for now you need to consider how to operate when not connected. This is about looking at Use Cases for your different types of user.

☒	Question	Why this matters
☐	8.2.18 Synchronization available offline and online?	What synchronization is there for the offline data with online data when the service is reconnected? Once you take data offline, there are now two versions. If the offline data is updated, how sophisticated is the service to synchronize it? Is this at a database, record or field level? How is conflict resolution handled? Does the capability vary by device? And at what cost?
☐	8.2.19 What offline data and access security?	What offline data and access security is provided by device? Theft or loss is a common problem for every mobile or portable device; laptops, PDA and phones. Once the corporate data is on these devices using the offline capability what security is there? Does the data automatically expire on a set date and 'evaporate'? Can a message be sent to the device that will "clear" the data?
☐	8.2.20 Is a phased approach for functionality acceptable?	Will the requirements be met in a later release in the roadmap of the service? Does the vendor have a track record of delivering on future functionality promises, and how are you going to deal with the interim workarounds? What happens if the vendor does not deliver?

☒	Question	Why this matters
☐	8.2.21 Roadmap for device support?	Are there devices that you have in the organization which are not supported, but are on their development roadmap? A roadmap is just that, with no promises of when and even if the capability will be provided. Do you need to get financial incentives into a contract around support for devices on the roadmap?
☐	8.2.22 What is the release strategy?	How are they going to release new functionality? And how are they going to inform you? The benefit of the Cloud Computing platform is that updates are implemented centrally. But how often? New releases could mean retraining. Lots of small releases may hint at a very unstable and patched service OR is it a very responsive vendor extending the service based on customer feedback.
☐	8.2.23 Which releases are still supported, and until when?	Can you even run on earlier release? Is this 'old-school' thinking? Maybe not. Not every Cloud Computing vendor is running a single instance (multi-tenanted) of their software for every customer. Enterprise software vendors offering their service as "Cloud Computing" may be running a separate instance for every customer in a VM (virtual management) environment, giving you flexibility of which releases you take.

☒	Question	Why this matters
☐	8.2.24 How many outstanding bugs and change requests?	What is the list of bugs that haven't been resolved? Do they distinguish between a bug and a change request? Which releases are they scheduled for? Do they matter to you? How many bugs are causing data problems? How many of the bugs will affect the area of functionality that you are planning to use? Do you have confidence that they will be resolved in the timeframes they have planned?
☐	8.2.25 Is there a well managed change cycle?	Can they describe how a bug or request for change makes it into the service? Do they have a controlled approach for registering and tracking change requests and bugs? How are you informed of new functionality? Are you notified when your change or bug is implemented?
	8.2.26 What is the vendors "track record" against key metrics?	Inevitably the focus will be on SLAs and there are questions in the legal section to support you there. But step back. What are the key metrics? It may not be response time but speed of availability of reports, data transfer or synchronizations. What is their track record in this area?

8.3 How is it delivered?

The end to end service is probably delivered by more than just the vendor, but this may not be very visible until you start digging. And once you start digging, where do you stop? And will you like what you find? However it is probably better to find out earlier in the project than when it all goes horribly wrong, and you have users screaming at you, the compliance team knocking at your door, and an uncomfortable meeting scheduled with the executive team.

However please remember that the amount of insight and information that either you will need or your vendor will provide will vary considerable depending on the nature of the service. There is a huge difference between outsourcing your company's ERP to a Cloud Computing service and using a free email account for a non critical service.

☒	Question	Why this matters
☐	8.3.1 What is the end to end service?	What are all the components of the complete end to end service? Some would argue that the beauty of a Cloud Computing service is that it is a "black box" that just works. Whilst there is merit in this, it has to be weighed against the relative immaturity of this market. There will be many factors that determine how far you dig, however….. Do you know what all the components of the service are? From design through development to delivery. Don't forget DR and back-up / restore. Wouldn't it be easier if the vendor had an end to end process map of their business which they could talk you through?
☐	8.3.2 Who provides the end to end service?	For every component in the end to end process, who actually provides the service, and under what contractual terms? It is unlikely that the vendor is providing all the elements of the service and so it is key to understand who they are sub-contracting to. Only then can you assess the risk based on the riskiest component. The most obvious is that very few vendors now run their own data centers. The exceptions are where they are so big that they can justify the massive investments e.g. IBM, Microsoft, or it is a hangover from previous investments when quality data center capacity was not readily available. You may be dealing with a small vendor, but if their services are delivered from a Tier 1 data center vendor then many of the risks are mitigated.

☒	Question	Why this matters
☐	8.3.3 What's the track record for components?	For each component, what are the capability, track record, contract and SLA of the vendor? How long term is the partnership or contract between the Cloud Computing vendor and the 3rd party vendor? There may be comfort from taking your service "direct" from the underlying vendor. However "partners" can often offer increased flexibility around commercial arrangements and customization offerings. Some of the commodity platform vendors are also acting as the data center vendor. Some work through partner networks and others are adopting a hybrid model. Examples of self hosting vendors are Google, Microsoft and Salesforce. But with all these 'moving parts' you need to be able to look your Cloud Computing vendor in the eye and know that they will underwrite the service SLAs. Or put another way 'One throat to choke'.
☐	8.3.4 What security processes and procedures are in place?	For each component, what security processes and procedures are followed? You should be looking for a clearly defined and documented security policy and ideally a recognized standard such as ISO27001. Your data is stored within the data center and you need to be confident that it is safe and people cannot simply walk in and take it or have uncontrolled access over the networks. But this is irrelevant if the backups are taken away by a taxi company to an insecure site. You should not ask a simple "Do you take security seriously YES/NO" question.

☒	Question	Why this matters
☐	8.3.5 Are operational processes followed?	For each component, what operational processes are followed? Are they documented adequately and version controlled? "I'm sure we have some Visio's on the intranet" is not good enough. You need to be looking for a clearly defined and documented policy and ideally a recognized approach such as ITIL. The adoption of a rigorous operational process, whilst no guarantee of success does indicate that the business takes operational excellence seriously.
☐	8.3.6 What is the Disaster Recovery approach?	What is their disaster recovery strategy and are the plans in place and up to date? Although unlikely, it is possible that a disaster will occur and the data center will effectively be out of action. You need to understand what provisions have been made (e.g. secondary data centers) and what the service levels for returning to operation are. Dependent upon the nature of the services you are using the speed of recovery may be critical. However you should be clear about the real consequences to your business for a service outage as the costs grow almost exponentially as you reduce the downtime.

☒	Question	Why this matters
☐	8.3.7 Can the DR, backup and restore be proven for customer audits and at what cost?	Can you (or your customers) audit the DR, backup and restore arrangements provided by the vendor? Can you attend disaster recovery rehearsal events or be actively engaged in data restore tests? Are there costs from the vendor associated with letting you or your customers be part of these activities? Of course depending on how many customers are "sharing" the service it may not be practical for the vendor to provide access to these events; however you can still ask them about the process and some sort of reporting.
☐	8.3.8 Who provides the DR, backup & restore?	The nature of the internet means that the data centers providing the service may not be located in your country or even geography. Therefore DR, back-up and restore may be more complex. You may have multiple vendors, one per region. For all of these you want to ensure that there is a credible company providing the service. You certainly don't want to find out that the DR site is a server in the CIO's home office and offsite backup means tapes taken home by the office manager.

☒	Question	Why this matters
☐	8.3.9 What redundancy exists within the data center?	Where are the points of failure and is there "engineered in" redundancy? Things do go wrong and how a data center handles this is key. Be clear about the details and quality of the response. Two cheap servers in separate office locations, connected by low cost broadband may be described as a "redundant network configuration with disaster recovery capabilities and high speed connectivity", however this may not be what you were expecting. Redundancy means no single points of failure, on-site spares, servers with failover both internally e.g. disks, and standby servers, multiple telecommunication vendors using separate circuits/wires and emergency power provision.
☐	8.3.10 Is it possible to run the service on-premise?	Although you are taking a Cloud Computing service because you didn't want to operate the s/w and associated infrastructure, there may be events that require you to change this position. If the vendor goes out of business or regulations in your industry change and make off-site data an unacceptable risk. One option is to ensure there is adequate Escrow provision. However escrow is not the magic bullet, you may get access to 500,000 lines of code, but are there instructions to compile or use the code and do you have the skills. It would be much better if the vendor provides a code base that can be installed either in the Cloud or on-premise e.g. Microsoft Dynamics CRM.

☒	Question	Why this matters
☐	8.3.11 How does the vendor test new releases?	Does the vendor provide a "non production" version of the service that would allow you to test new releases before the new release is rolled out? You wouldn't implement a major new system in house without User Acceptance Testing, so why should this be different for Cloud Computing? Can you contribute to the vendors in-house testing of new versions? This may provide a way for you to shape the service to your specific needs?
☐	8.3.12 What data clean up tools are available?	Cleaning your existing data prior to migration is a key step for success. Does your vendor or a 3rd party provide such tools? If so what confidence do you have that they work accurately, can you see evidence of previous use e.g. references or case studies? Even with this comfort, you should still consider "desk checking" a representative sample in advance.
☐	8.3.13 What migration tools are available?	The vendor or 3rd parties may have tools that simplify the migration from your existing service. This is a critical step and you will want to be confident it will work. Get evidence of others who have used the tools successfully and what lessons they learnt. Even with this you should build in manual checks to ensure the tools have worked as expected.

☒	Question	Why this matters
☐	8.3.14 What internal DR and roll-back processes are in place during migration?	During the migration from your existing on-premise solution to the new Cloud service, things may not go smoothly. What DR or roll-back procedures do you need to have in place internally? This is the point of maximum risk, the transition from your systems to their service. Assume that it won't work, or there will be problems. That means having some DR and roll-back plans in place.
☐	8.3.15 What is the release schedule?	How often are releases? How much input and warning do you get to plan. In this new Cloud Computing world the benefit for the vendor is they can update the software easily. This also means that you always have the latest release with all of its new functionality. However the downside is that you have a potential control nightmare. Suddenly your service has new functionality which you have not prepared your user base for.
☐	8.3.16 Are new releases mandatory?	Do you get the option of not implementing new releases? Are there tools or facilities in the service which allows you to control what new functionality is seen by users? Can you even run on earlier release? Is this 'old-school' thinking? Maybe not. Not every Cloud Computing vendor is running a single instance (multi-tenanted) of their software for every customer. Enterprise software vendors offering their service as "Cloud Computing" may be running a separate instance for every customer in a VM (virtual management) environment.

☒	Question	Why this matters
☐	8.3.17 How do you test new releases before go-live?	This will include both the vanilla release and the customizations or configurations, for all devices. More mature Cloud Computing services have a 'sandbox' which is used for testing. Alternatively are there parallel services that can be used for testing, but at a far lower cost? And every device needs testing. Suddenly the customizations are looking expensive. And do you have confidence that configurations are unaffected so that you don't need to test….. I thought not.
☐	8.3.18 Are releases rolled-out by device or region?	The worst of all worlds is the announcement 'Global roll-out' with 'to the USA only' buried in the small print. Multi-lingual implementations are hard. But if you are planning a truly global roll-out, take a long hard look at this issue.
☐	8.3.19 Are there tools provided to migrate between releases?	Are the tools robust enough with roll-back capabilities? Any data schema change will require a migration of some sort. Remember migration is the highest risk time. How often is the Cloud Computing vendor going to put you through that?

☒	Question	Why this matters
☐	8.3.20 What impact will a new release have on your Customization's?	Has their release strategy thought through the issues of configuration and customization? Have they been through enough release cycles? Have they enough customers to understand the different combinations of configuration and customization. You don't control the release schedule, they do. Don't get into a position where you are "held hostage" and put your business at risk or spend enormous amounts to mitigate that risk.
☐	8.3.21 Is there a community offering customizations and add-ons?	Is this exchange or marketplace managed by the vendor or by a 3rd party? The more active the add-on community the more likely you are to find the add-on that meets your specific needs and the less you are likely to pay for it. But it does require customization capabilities of the commodity services and availability of developer API's. But for every add-on there is another company where you need to understand their capabilities and risk.
☐	8.3.22 How established is the partner ecosystem?	Being a partner of a vendor varies massively. The greatest difference is how difficult and expensive it is to become a partner. The more difficult, the lower the risk to you. How do partners qualify and reach new levels? How rigorous is the assessment? Is it worth anything?
☐	8.3.23 What validation or certification is there for 3rd party services?	Does the vendor or an external body manage partner certification of add-ons? Is the validation valid? Does the certification body have teeth? Do they fail products, and if so what happens?

☒	Question	Why this matters
☐	8.3.24 What online training tools and self service support are provided?	The typically low revenue per user in the Cloud model means that the vendor cannot afford to have the user contacting them on a regular basis. To reduce the need for customers to call the "helpdesk" and to increase the use of a service, vendors will normally provide online tools. The breadth, depth and quality of the tools vary massively.

8.4 What are the commercial arrangements?

Every vendor needs to be paid for delivering a service (even if not directly from you e.g. ad funding, freemium or sponsorship) and there are many ways to structure the deal. Some will suit you and your budgeting and accounting model better than others. In some situations the vendor will be prepared to negotiate and bend, in others they cannot or will not.

A vendors approach to the commercial arrangements can be driven by where they have come from. A startup Cloud Computing service will have no legacy. All their contracts will be new and written for the new business. Their revenue models will probably be based on monthly annuity revenue and their investors will know and be fully supportive of this.

However a more mature vendor with an existing on premise business will need to consider how the changes to the Cloud affect their cash flow compared to their existing "up front" revenue model. Or how their sales compensation plans will need to alter and how to ensure that their existing customers do not feel they have overpaid. This can lead vendors to model the Cloud pricing to their existing models i.e. upfront fees, long term (2 or 3 year) contract periods and incentives for you to pay everything up front. Although not considered to be "normal" Cloud commercial arrangements, these may work for you.

Some vendors are 100% hosted and will never license the system to be run on your servers (on-premise). Others however may be more flexible, using Cloud Computing as the easy entry point into your organization with the longer term aim being an enterprise on-premise solution.

☒	Question	Why this matters
☐	8.4.1 What is the vendor's sales model?	Of all the different types of sales models, which are available from the vendor? Monthly, quarterly, named user, volume and usage based, freemium, ad funded, open source? How flexible are they? Which payment approach suits your preferred investment profile? Understanding how a vendor is intending to interact with you will help set your expectations for some of the questions below. For example with a "free/ad funded" mass market offering, it is unlikely that you will be able to vary contract terms or have access to a personal sales rep. You will need to understand from the web site literature what the offering is and then decide if it fits with your requirements.
☐	8.4.2 What is the basis for pricing?	What drives the vendor's revenue model? What are the sensitivities, and will this affect (or compromise) how you decide to use the service? This is an obvious question; however there are many variations and it can often be difficult to compare apples with apples. There are variable costs as far as the vendor is concerned e.g. bandwidth, storage etc. and they need to find a way to cover these costs. Traditionally software has been sold as a perpetual license with an optional annual maintenance charge. The Cloud model has opened up different opportunities for monetizing the service offered. Can you scale up and down, or is it a ratchet?

☒	Question	Why this matters
☐	8.4.3 What payment schedules are available?	How are payments scheduled in the contract; monthly, quarterly, once a threshold cost reached etc? For budgeting purposes you need to have a cost schedule. Just because the service is advertised as a $x/month cost, that doesn't mean that the service is paid monthly. Vendors may charge for 12 months in advance.
☐	8.4.4 Are there minimum contract periods and lock-ins?	What is the initial lock-in period, and what are the break clauses and penalties? Often the vendor requires an initial 12 month contract. It may take you 6 months to implement the solution and discoverer that it doesn't work for you. What clauses are there to break the contract and get a refund?
☐	8.4.5 How is the "free" service funded?	How can the vendor continue to offer the service, if it appears to be free? You need to dig into their business model to really understand why it is sustainable.
☐	8.4.6 What are the hidden costs of a free service?	Does the free service stop and under what terms? This may not matter if you are using the service for trial or limited length project. But trials have a nasty habit of suddenly becoming mainstream and then strategic, without any due diligence.

☒	Question	Why this matters
☐	8.4.7 In what areas and on what basis will the vendor negotiate discounts?	Do they need reference sites? Do they need cash, so annual up-front vs. monthly? Do they need security of revenue stream, so a longer contract is appealing? Is making an investment in the company an option? The smaller the company, the more likely they are to negotiate on terms. Alternatively they may want to break into a new market or industry. Do your research on their future plans. Then, be creative. You may be surprised what they will give you if you are prepared to negotiate creatively.
☐	8.4.8 Are there setup and/or one-off fees?	Although the headline charges are typically the monthly subscription fees, there may be one off charges at the outset of the agreement. These may help to reduce the monthly fee as the vendor has been able to reduce their fixed costs of service. However you need to understand these and be able to compare the costs across the contract period to another vendor who has no upfront fees. If both vendors are offering the same service then the costs will be included somewhere. Is this how they fund the company whilst they wait for the recurring revenue to build? However, upfront fees should not be assumed to be bad. These charges may align to your business needs e.g. training or vendor adoption services and may make the transition to the Cloud model more effective. The key is to be very clear about what they are and how you will benefit from them.

☒	Question	Why this matters
☐	8.4.9 Data clean up and migration costs?	What involvement and costs is required for data clean up and migration? Unless you are a greenfield site you will have data to migrate. Now could be the time to clean up the duplication and archive old data. But can you do this or is there a 3rd party cost? Have they experience of migrating data in the volume and complexity that you have?
☐	8.4.10 What are the support costs, by region at the different SLA levels?	Support costs vary massively, from free (i.e. included) to cost-per-call. Open source companies make much of their money on premium support. For others it is a part of the monthly cost. If the support level is compromised outside core hours, then you should be paying 'off-peak' rates. Alternatively plan to develop your own Center of Excellence (CoE), but make sure this is reflected in the price. Maybe you can offer the CoE to other customers for a fee.
☐	8.4.11 Are there additional costs for support?	What additional costs are there for 'out of hours' or on-site support, by region? Are you getting the value for the additional costs vs. establishing a CoE?
☐	8.4.12 What are the costs for training?	What are the options for training by region, by device, by service offering and what are the costs? Don't get fooled into, "It's an intuitive web based application. You don't need training". It is an implementation of a business system. Cloud Computing just means someone else is running it.

☒	Question	Why this matters
☐	8.4.13 What are the costs for tailoring training?	Are you even able to reuse or buy the IP to tailor the training? Do you have to get the vendor to do it for you? Is there a 3rd party market for training that will drive "value"? There is the cost of the training material, but how does your company charge for the opportunity cost of people not working, for trainers and for training facilities?
☐	8.4.14 What are the costs for customization?	Who can develop the customizations and test them? The cost of customization is a one-off, however there may then be a recurring cost for every new release to implement and test. Customizations should be avoided wherever possible. If customizations are necessary then have you selected the right service?
☐	8.4.15 What limits upside costs?	If the service is volume based is there a headline cap? What can you put in place, or what tools are provided, to monitor and limit the total cost? Procurement departments hate any contract where the costs could be unlimited. And as the usage of the service is probably difficult to predict any volume or usage based service is probably impossible to budget accurately. What will your approach be?
☐	8.4.16 Are there additional costs based on data volumes or usage?	This is typically the 'freemium' model. The base version is free, but to get additional capability, disk space, bandwidth, no advertising, then you need to upgrade to paid version.

☒	Question	Why this matters
☐	8.4.17 Additional users during migration?	Can you have additional users for set-up and migration and then revert to normal levels post implementation? For development, testing and roll-out you may have more licenses than required for steady state. How are you going to be charged for them?
☐	8.4.18 Is an Ad funded service appropriate?	Is an ad-funded model appropriate for your staff and any 3rd parties that access the service? If someone is entering this month's customer invoices should they have adverts presented to distract them? Or in the education sector should a service for children have adverts? There is a lot of industry buzz about ad funded services, largely driven by the incredible success of Google. Ad funding is normally linked to "free" however it is probably better to compare it to our experiences with the media where for example we have newspapers being variously free or subsidized by the revenue generated from advertising.
☐	8.4.19 In an ad funded service is there control over the adverts presented?	What control is there over the ads; inappropriate, competition, recruiters etc? Is this control down to region or user type? What happens if inappropriate adverts slip through their filters? If you are implementing internally – avoid. Find another service, pay to remove the ads, negotiate them out, or skip to the next section.
☐	8.4.20 Missing SLAs refunds?	If they miss any SLAs how are these identified, and how are refunds provided? Are they service credits or hard cash?

☒	Question	Why this matters
☐	8.4.21 Service credits?	If the vendor fails to meet the SLAs what are the credits or refunds that you are given and how are they triggered? Does vendor have mechanisms in place to report SLAs? Do you? If they are uncomfortable with this, then you need to question their confidence that they can hit their SLA targets. You should also have a mechanism to measure their SLAs and a process internally to trigger a discount. Don't expect the vendor to have the monitoring in place. Does the service credit really compensate you for the lack of service? Be clear about what the percentage target for acceptable availability actually means e.g. 365x24 = 8760 hours, 99% means 87.6 hrs or 3.65 days downtime. But if all the downtime happened within working hours then an outage of 87.6hrs/8 = 11 working days (or 2 working weeks) would still be within SLA!
	8.4.22 Other customers with favorable terms?	Are there customers with more favorable terms and contractually can you demand the provider matches them?
☐	8.4.23 Other customers with special arrangements?	Are there other customers that have negotiated special terms or conditions that could affect your level of service? i.e. a major customer who demands a shutdown quarterly for full backup, or can delay new releases.

8.5 What legals do I need to consider?

The following comments are not intended to provide any type of formal legal guidance and if you have concerns regarding aspects of any contract between yourself and a vendor then you should seek professional legal advice.

Disclaimer made (!!), our hope is that this section will start you thinking about the Smart Questions. This should save you some time with lawyers and hopefully reduce your legal bills.

☒	Question	Why this matters
☐	8.5.1 Is there a single point of Contract? (n.b. not contact!!)	It is possible there will be multiple parties involved with the provision of the service. You do not want to be chasing all these parties on contractual matters. Ideally you want a single party that you contract with. This reduces the opportunity for "passing the blame" or for conflicting arrangements between one party's contract and the next.
☐	8.5.2 Are the SLA's and associated penalties included as negotiated?	SLAs (Service Level Agreements) are at the very heart of the provisioning of the service. Are the following included; when the service is available, allowed downtime, acceptable exceptions, performance of the networks and how quickly the helpdesk will respond, how long to get the DR site up and running? These may vary by region, service and device. When everything is working well you will not look at your SLAs but if things go wrong they are your key vehicle to get things resolved. There is a clear link between the quality of the operational procedures and security policies a data center follows and the quality of the SLA's. Take a hard look at the SLAs against your business requirements.

☒	Question	Why this matters
☐	8.5.3 Are there "Acceptable Use" clauses?	Many contracts include some form of "acceptable use" clause that is intended to provide the vendor with the option to "talk to the customer" in the event that the customer starts doing something that was unforeseen or unplanned e.g. finding a way to store huge volumes of data on the service when this was never intended and not formally contracted for. If the "acceptable use" clause is too central to "the contract" then you are open for lots of "discussions" with the vendor and sudden increases in charges or requests for you to leave.
☐	8.5.4 What termination clauses are included?	It is only fair that both parties have options to terminate the agreement, however they should be balanced. What notice periods are required, are they "without cause" etc?
☐	8.5.5 What "transfer of rights" are in the contract?	Many Cloud Computing vendors will have an exit strategy based on being purchased by a bigger player. To ensure that this is easy for the purchaser they may include some form of right to pass on your contract. This could be a good thing, with a larger player providing greater funding, and a wider range of services and facilities. However it may result in work or challenges for you. Do you need to "risk assess" the new owner? Is the new owner going to consolidate the service in a new data center that may be out of your geography and create data ownership issues? Does the new owner present your company with issues from a political, ethical or even legal perspective?

☒	Question	Why this matters
☐	8.5.6 Is there a clearly defined Dispute management process?	In the event of a dispute does the contract help you get what you need? If the vendor is in another country is it worth pursuing them and under what laws? If the service is really two guys in a bedroom, or the vendor has an obscure offshore address, how easy and worthwhile is it to take legal action. What benefit are you going to get? Far better to plan for the worst before you sign-up for the service – "Plan for the divorce, not the honeymoon". And remember that disputes can go both ways, the vendor may decide that they have a dispute with you. What is the notification period for remedy and are there any "3 strikes and you are out clauses" There should be an "ultimate authority" that can be used to resolve disputes where you and the vendor have failed to reach agreement yourselves. Who is this and are they a credible organization.
☐	8.5.7 During dispute, time to migrate to alternative service?	If there is a dispute, does the contract give you sufficient time to migrate to an alternative service? If it took you 3 months to implement the solution, then how long will it take you to migrate and at what risk to the smooth operation of the organization. Are there provisions that ensure that the vendor will assist you in this process?

☒	Question	Why this matters
☐	8.5.8 How is "data ownership" handled in contract?	What provisions are in your contract for data ownership? What rights do you have during the contract? What happens at the end of the contract or if you breach any terms? How do you get copies and in what formats? What rights has the vendor included to allow them to handle your data e.g. for backups? The data should always be yours, but out of sight should not be out of mind. Be clear about your rights to copies of the data to store yourself (even if this is a chargeable service). What happens if the vendor goes out of business, how quickly can you have a backup of your data so you can find another service vendor, and in what formats. Even if you have a copy of the data do you need proprietary tools that only the vendor has access to in order to read the data?
☐	8.5.9 Are there geographical implications in the contract?	What rights do the local authorities have to access the data, by region? Depending on the location of the data center the rights of the local authorities to access your data will differ.
☐	8.5.10 What is the legal jurisdiction of the contract?	You may be based and be using the service from the UK; however the vendor may be based in France. What legal jurisdiction has authority over the contract you sign? Some vendors provide a single contract globally with a single legal jurisdiction, others offer contracts tailored to the region of use. Make sure that you understand the implications of this – you may not have access to legal skills for Uzbekistan!!!!

☒	Question	Why this matters
☐	8.5.11 Are there any "Step in" rights within the contract?	Are there rights that allow a 3rd party to "step in" and run the service in the event that the vendor has difficulties? Clearly you need to be aware of this, but it may not be a problem. Maybe the vendors hosting partner wants the option to keep running the service "as is" in the event that the vendor goes under, so that they can a) keep the end customer (you) happy b) reduce the chance of you suing them for lack of service now the vendor has gone or c) generate some revenue to offset their costs as the service is wound down or a new owner found.
☐	8.5.12 How do you terminate the service?	Even if everything has gone to plan and the service has met your needs, at some point you may wish to leave the service. It is a good idea to agree up front how this will work. How do you get copies of your data? Are there any costs for this and what support will the vendor provide to assist in you planned departure?
☐	8.5.13 Can you get visibility through the vendor to their key suppliers?	Most vendors will be using a number of 3rd parties to provide the services. It is normal for the vendor to "back to back" any contractual commitments they make. The risk is that your vendor promises the earth to you, but has no contractual way to get this from their 3rd parties e.g. Service Levels at 100% to you, but nothing better than 99.9% from the data center.

☒	Question	Why this matters
☐	8.5.14 How can you gain early warning of vendor failure?	What do you need to put in place to monitor and get early warning of termination of the service? Tracking the annual accounts of the vendor and key suppliers, monitoring SLAs, getting to know the management team, taking a stake in the company. For larger vendors e.g. IBM, Microsoft it can help to follow journalists and commentators who specialize in that vendor. They will often provide early visibility to changes, even if these are "unofficial".
☐	8.5.15 Is the vendor's code in escrow?	What escrow provisions are in the contract? Is the vendor providing this as part of the service or expecting you to pay on an "as needs" basis. Although escrow may appear to be a sensible option it can be worthless unless you have the skills (or can acquire the skills) to step in. However if escrow is the right thing for you then consider how often is code placed in escrow and what proof is there that it is "good" code. Is there a 3rd party verification process that the code in escrow can be compiled?
☐	8.5.16 How do you gain access to "code in escrow"?	Are the processes to get the code from escrow clearly documented, and how do you initiate it? What are the rules that determine release (no good if there is a 6 month wait!!)?
☐	8.5.17 What skills do you need to be able to use the escrow code?	So now you have 1,000,000 lines of undocumented code in 348 files spread across 27 folders. Now what? What development skills, development tools and delivery infrastructure do you need to get the system up and running?

☒	Question	Why this matters
☐	8.5.18 What is the cost of implementing the escrow code?	If it was required how much would it cost and how long would it take, conservatively to take the code and get it running? Can you get access to staff from the vendor? They may have just lost their jobs and be very happy to provide services to help you.
☐	8.5.19 What alternative options for maintaining the service are there?	It may be better to have an option to keep paying for the service in its current state directly with the data center. Are there other customers who are better placed to run the service? Do you know them? Would owning an equity stake in the vendor give you more warning and more control?

Chapter

9

Funny you should say that...

Laughter gives us distance. It allows us to step back from an event, deal with it and then move on.

Bob Newhart (Comedian, 1929 –)

CLOUD Computing sounds great in theory and we trust that the previous chapters of questions have been helpful. However we appreciate that the structure of question followed by question, may not have been an exciting or fun read. What the book is missing are some stories or anecdotes which bring the Smart Questions to life.

Now life isn't always fun. Some of the stories are painful and expensive. But that makes them all the more valuable.

If we'd interspersed these stories with the questions it would have made the last Chapters too long. It would also have prevented you using the questions as checklists or aide-memoires. So we've grouped together our list of stories in this Chapter. I'm sure that you have your own stories – both positive and negative - so let us know them:

stories@Smart-Questions.com

Quick to access means quick to implement. Right?

CRM is one of the most visible Cloud Computing services, but implementing a CRM solution means getting sales teams to follow consistent processes and conform in the way that they enter customer and order data. Now it isn't an impossible task, but it is up there with pushing water uphill with a sieve. So, Cloud Computing isn't going to make this job any easier. The reduction in the project costs – often 40-50% saving – is only in the software element of the implementation. Don't be fooled into thinking that they same savings can be made in the implementation services. These will take just as long and cost just as much as it does with a traditional on-premise app. Why would it be any different?

Consumer apps are sneaking into corporates.

Skype, Facebook, Twitter, GoogleApps – and they are just the well known ones. For every one of these there are literally hundreds of small vendors out there fulfilling a niche. How many of these, aided and abetted by Cloud Computing are making it into your corporation? Now, that is no bad thing. Innovation is good. However innovative apps which become the "de facto" standard without any due diligence are bad.

What is your formal process for getting an application onto a user's desktop? Big corporates have locked down desktops, which is great for control but stifles innovation. Outsourced service providers make their money by rigidly controlling change. A major supermarket's IT department was so responsive that they were a runaway cost. They would implement anything and everything the users wanted. For them, the benefits promised by the outsourced service providers were almost entirely achieved by saying "No" to innovation and sticking to the agreed program of change.

Who is more dangerous than you?

You may be well organized, secure and safe. But who is within 2 miles of you that could shut your business down. Who could take out your power supply, your communications, or force the area to be evacuated? Take a look on GoogleMaps or LiveMaps. There was a small data center within the World Trade Center complex prior to 9/11. What they didn't know was that 3 stories below them were 200,000 liters of diesel for the Port of New York Emergency Generator.

A UK data capture agency has their primary site less than 10 miles from a major oil refinery, but their back-up site is less than 5 miles from the same threat. If there was an incident the back-up would be compromised first.

Even legacy application vendors can play.

But Cloud Computing is not just for mega-corporations. Nimbus was founded as a traditional enterprise software vendor where the software was developed and then shipped on a CD. But they found a barrier to selling their innovative process mapping software was the customer's IT department who could take 6 months to find a server and install the software. Now with a Cloud Computing offering, and without rewriting the suite of software, a customer can be using the software immediately. As a result Nimbus' revenues are growing at 40% year on year.

Gets you out of a hole.

Adopting a Cloud-intensive IT strategy can be a matter of timing and simple math. The new CIO took the post at a subsidiary of a global manufacturer just six months before the business was to be spun off as an independent private company. They were given 15 months to extract themselves from the parent's IT environment—a very tall order. "Cloud Computing has been perfect for us," says the CIO. "We're trying to keep our IT staff as small as possible, and I want the people we do have, to work on business support issues, not infrastructure."

The answer is no. What was your question?

An off-shore investment bank on a small Caribbean island was very robust during its audit. No CCTV was installed. No PhotoID for employees. No visitor badges: "we don't have visitors" No intruder detection: "we don't have burglars". No security training. No smoke detectors: "we don't have fires". No UPS or generator: "we don't have power cuts". The business continuity plan and Disaster Recovery plan is on the same island: "we don't have hurricanes".

It is too expensive to do it right.

A large multinational service vendor had sites in the UK, in Germany and other European countries. The UK had no idea how to do encryption, but the Germany site did. The UK couldn't 'tap' into Germany's knowledge because they would charge the UK site at commercial rates and this made it too expensive, although there was a $1 million contract at risk.

One of their UK sites had got CCTV but it was black and white analog nearing the end of its life, and the system date and time was wrong so it might not have been much use in a court case. Neither of the UK sites gave their Employees a PhotoID, even though they had 450 & 620 employees respectively, so they couldn't argue everyone knew each other and would spot a stranger. All of these could be spotted in a simple site visit.

I wish I had known, I wish I had asked...

The most common problems CIOs encounter come when they discover that they've entrusted the maintenance and management of their software to people who lack the industry expertise needed to run a mission-critical application. This is precisely the realization the CIO of a national home builder has come to about the Cloud Computing arena, and now he wishes he'd had a clearer idea of what factors to consider before he leapt into the Cloud.

At first, everything seemed to go as expected. All the needed features and functions were in place, and those that weren't often were added by the vendor at his request. But he fell into the same trap other CIOs are falling into: he focused too much on those features and functions and how they matched up with business needs, when he should have been looking more closely at how the system would perform during periods of high demand or when the vendor was updating the application.

"When I have a two-hour outage in a mission-critical application, I can't accept an answer from the provider that's an 'oops,'" he says. "If I ran my shop the way they run this application, I would have been fired."

Business systems are not the IT dept's playground.

Despite being a company of just 400 employees, a publisher was relying on two databases, two e-commerce systems and three workflow systems to support its three brands. The new CEO decreed that the company, which depends on technology for its existence, would consolidate on one platform.

Naturally, the IT department saw that as an invitation to roll up its sleeves, and it specified a home-grown solution that was doomed from the get-go. "I didn't doubt that they could do it, but we're a company that wanted to move very quickly," the CEO says. His decision to move to Cloud Computing was immediately, and eerily, validated. "The morning we made our decision, our IT system went down for four hours," he recalls. "Somebody was telling me we were doing the right thing."

Where exactly is your data center and backup?

For a European airline their data center is within airport perimeter. Daily back-ups are held in fireproof safe, but inside the computer room. If there was a civil aviation disaster, who would volunteer to run back in to open the safe? Monthly back-ups were held offsite in "the bunker". On closer questioning it turned out to be a surplus concrete hut 100m away - on the flight path. So with an airline crash the back-ups might be the first thing to go. When asked about Disaster Recovery their approach was "there might be a plan, but it would only be communicated to us in the event of an incident arising".

All data is classified as secret.

One UK government department tried to implement a Cloud Computing solution, but had to go through its outsourced service provider. But the outsourced service provider had no interest in letting another supplier take a piece of the action. They had every opportunity to make it difficult for the new vendor and very, very expensive for the customer. They simply wheeled in their security expert and then their commercial manager with a handful of Change Request forms.

Cue the data security team. These are the guys that are ignored for years, and suddenly this is their chance to wield their power, however irresponsibly. Their initial response that ALL data was secret so couldn't be held on the Cloud Computing solution. Then it was pointed out that some of the data was brochures and documents which were designed for the public and available on the public facing website.

Responsible risk-taking

The VP of Product Development saw an opportunity to experiment with using Cloud Computing to host a digital media company's online communities. He could evaluate the impact on performance, usage and a host of other measurable indicators. He also deduced that relying on Cloud Computing resources would allow his group to become more entrepreneurial, because their efforts wouldn't create drag on the performance of other systems.

Because the community offerings are all relatively new, venturing into the Cloud wouldn't require a big migration project. But before he could take the plunge, he had to be certain the Cloud - which would provide metered, on-demand computing power and data storage – could conform to the company's culture of "responsible risk-taking." That meant a healthy dose of due diligence.

How long can you survive?

How far away is their Disaster Recovery site? You may need to get your staff there to work at it, and you will probably need to be able to get their within the hour. So less than 25 miles, so commuting long term is a possibility, without losing staff or burning them out. But it needs to be outside the Emergency Exclusion Zone. After 9/11 a major bank didn't get back into its New York HQ for over 6 months.

Do you even know where their data center and DR site is?

Strategy by the back door?

A major US State Department came to the Cloud more by happenstance than by design. They never made a decision to adopt a Cloud strategy; rather, they simply started looking at Cloud Computing alternatives whenever the IT staff had processing needs that the existing resources couldn't accommodate, or if they saw an opportunity to significantly cut application-related costs.

More often than not, the Cloud Computing option made more sense than any other choice. "If anything," the CIO says, "speed to market drove it initially, and then the recognition of the much more manageable costs has driven it further."

Once they identify a service they are interested in, they perform some due diligence, working with the vendor to verify that the security of data—at rest and in transfer—is sufficient. They look for services that have built-in redundancy and strong disaster recovery processes, an important consideration in based on their location. They also make sure access to data is guaranteed around the clock, and check on the location of data storage to make sure citizen records don't end up on overseas servers.

There is a better way.

Three years ago, when the new CIO joined a very large company that manages hospital emergency departments and physicians, he immediately noted the amount of time his staff spent writing application code and maintaining the infrastructure to support it. He knew there had to be a better way.

"I walked into the CEO's office," he recalls, "and said, 'Do you want to be a software development company, or do you want to be a medical management company supported by software?'"

That question jump-started the company's journey into the IT phenomenon known as Cloud Computing. Three years after signing on to a Cloud Computing CRM service they estimate that half of the business processes the IT staff support now happen in the Cloud.

In the future, it won't matter where your software lives. "As a matter of fact, if you have it on premise, you're short-changing yourself, because you're throwing half of your resources at supporting the server infrastructure".

Or maybe not.

The following is a genuine stream of Tweets from a Web2.0 Twitter add-on provider. Note that their nightmare start 25th December and ends 3rd February. But the early warning came on 2nd Dec with the statement, "having some growing pains"

Can your company continue with an outage like this from your Cloud Computing vendor?

Twitter stream – a cautionary tale

Having some growing pains, thanks for your patience folks, emails will come just a little delayed 6:55 2nd Dec

Doing some server maintenance over the next day or so, sorry for no alerts, but you shouldn't be working any way. :) 8:48am 25th Dec

Server maintenance has been a nightmare, and not easy during big holiday, sorry folks. New servers arrive Monday, will be up and going then. 10:39 28th Dec

Had our main server die, backups ended up not working, recovering from a raid 5 hard drive system, taking longer than we hoped 10:33 pm 6th Jan

Getting closer to being online, but probably a couple more days out, thanks for your patience 10:41pm 6th Jan

Coming back soon, just a little longer! thanks! 6:45am 16th Jan

Hopefully end of the week, the data recovery company is painfully slow! 8:18pm 27th Jan

We're back and better than ever with new servers and a new server admin! 11:32am 3rd Feb

---

Chapter

Final Word

A conclusion is the place where you got tired of thinking.

Albert Bloch (American Artist, 1882 – 1961)

B Y column inch Cloud Computing probably gets more coverage than any other aspect of IT. Pros and cons. Technical approaches. Blatant adverts dressed up as case studies.

But this is one area of IT that is still evolving fast. Maturing, rather than matured. That means there are plenty of opportunities to gain competitive advantage, and also there are also risks in the same proportion.

Regardless of one's views on the readiness of Cloud Computing to meet corporate IT needs, it's a development that cannot be ignored. Like it or not, the idea of renting applications, development platforms, processing power, storage or any other Cloud-enabled services has emerged as a consequence of the Internet's rise as a business tool. It's a potentially game-changing technology that's expected to reshape IT over the next decade.

By asking the Smart Questions you can take a realistic, balanced view of the potential gains and opportunities and consider them in the context of the operational, legal and compliance risks.

And remember, once you've asked the questions the decision may be "No".

Appendix: Book Summary

Common Approach, Uncommon Results

Tackle the biggest barrier to performance – adoption of your improvement initiatives. By everyone in the company. The easy way. Today.

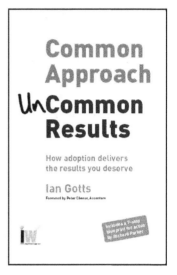

Common Approach UnCommon Results

How adoption delivers the results you deserve

Ian Gotts

Foreword by Peter Cheese, Accenture

'Common Approach – Uncommon Results' reveals a proven approach which is simple and practical, and achieves staggering levels of adoption. It comes from the day-to-day experience working with more than 500 organizations, including Lockheed Martin, Orange, Toyota, and Accenture BPO.

How do you really deliver results on all the initiatives and projects in your company? The answer is Adoption. Through Adoption, everyone in your company ensures that your strategy gets implemented and you obtain visible results from your initiative.

We put this succinctly: $R=IA^2$ (Results = Initiatives x Adoption^2)

Maximizing Results by successful Adoption of the transformational changes driven out of the Initiatives. In other words, it does not matter how many initiatives (projects, exercises, and programs, whatever) you throw at people if no one adopts the results of them. Typical initiatives include Six Sigma, software implementation (SAP, Siebel etc), Cost Reduction, Sarbanes Oxley and outsourcing programs.

While this may sound obvious, the corporate landscape is rife with these initiatives in progress, where little or no thought has been put into how to make sure that the rest of the organization actually adopt and own whatever improvement is advocated. Little surprise then that the adoption rate (and hence the success rate) of initiatives is pitifully low in many companies.

Gaining adoption is a challenge, not least because it involves changes in behavior and attitudes. Inspirational leadership helps kick-start adoption throughout the company, but it cannot sustain the necessary continuous improvement required for companies to stay competitive. Adoption has measurable results, as the dramatic benefits obtained by the success stories reveal.

Adoption means communicating the changes required of people – and getting people to make the changes. The approach we are suggesting is applicable to virtually every initiative and it is achievable as it makes change as painless as possible. This is where a common language is required – an operational language which can describe the changes in activities, behavior and results that are expected.

This language describes activities, roles and measures, and is managed through the use of an Intelligent Operations Manual (IOM). It manages processes, documents, resources and metrics – and the relationships between them. This is made possible by current IT infrastructure and software. Use of this IOM enhances accountability and serves to further adoption. And once the IOM is in place it can be applied to other initiatives and therefore increases their return on investment.

Whilst this may seem interesting in practice, most companies already have a range of initiative s at different stages. Therefore the book takes 5 typical initiatives (outsourcing, Six Sigma, software package implementation, compliance and rapid growth) and considers the most effective way of implementing the IOM alongside them depending on the phase of the initiative.

From the experience of countless customer engagements we have identified 7 simple steps to develop and manage the Common Operational Platform. These steps build on the principles of Adoption, but sets them out in a practical blueprint for action.

Once you will have gone through these steps, it will be remarkable how the barriers to change seem to disappear. It even keeps the strategy and your objectives to the fore when a business faces rapid growth.

Achieving results – the easy way. Turning your strategy into reality.

Comments about the book

"The book addresses the question that all business managers have been struggling with over the past years: how are all these initiatives and projects going to work together. The answer is offered in a simple and practical way. As a reader you truly get the feeling that you can do something with the tips and solutions that are suggested."

Manager, Strategic Projects Group - Toyota Motor Marketing Europe

"His tone is well judged and witty enough to make the book a delight to read."

Computer Business Review

Out of guilt I have plunged in and just completed Parts I and II, and enjoyed both the written style and the illuminating content. Thankfully, as ever, the best advice is always common sense, but so often businesses and senior management complicate matters (frequently, sadly, with input from management consultants...).

Partner, Accenture, UK

You can actually measure the success of a strategy by looking at what the whole company is focused on (or not). The approach Ian suggests makes this simple concept accessible by involving everyone in the building of a common understanding, with impressive results. The most refreshing business book I've read in a long time."

Marketing Director, Capita, UK

Notes pages

Notes pages